YOU CAN OVERCOME ANYTHING!

VOL.13

WITH COURAGE

CESAR R. ESPINO WITH CONTRIBUTING AUTHORS

WITH A SPECIAL CHAPTER BY

DAVID SELVIN

Copyright © 2024 by Cesar R. Espino

All rights reserved. No part of this publication may be reproduced, distributed, or transmitted in any form or by any means, without prior written permission from the publisher.

Published by Cesar R. Espino / CRE Companies

You Can Overcome Anything! Vol.13 / Cesar R. Espino With Contributing Authors – 1ST Ed.

ISBN: 978-1-960665-18-8 (dBook)
ISBN: 978-1-960665-17-1 (pbk)

www.CesarRespino.com

DEDICATION

This book is dedicated to those seeking inspiration, motivation, and empowerment; to those striving to achieve more in life, understanding that courage is key. By cultivating courage, one can apply the lessons learned to confront life's obstacles and overcome them. It is my belief that within these pages, you will discover stories from various authors that will aid you on your personal journey. Through these narratives, you will find ideas and real-life lessons demonstrating how you too can truly **Overcome Anything!**

CONTENTS

ACKNOWLEDGEMENTS i

David Selvin – Chapter One — 1
ATTRACTING GOOD LIFE THROUGH COURAGEOUS ENDEAVORS

Judy Sweeney – Chapter Two — 13
COURAGE: HAVING FEAR AND DOING IT ANYWAY

Mike Kroupa – Chapter Three — 25
A LIFELONG JOURNEY OF GROWTH AND DISCOVERY

Cortney Vaughn – Chapter Four — 39
FROM DESPAIR TO DESTINY

COURAGE, FORGIVENESS, AND FREEDOM COVERS IT ALL

Duffy Ford – Chapter Five — 49
CREATING A GREAT LIFE WITH COURAGEOUS SMALL STEPS

Po Lin Grealy – Chapter Six — 63
STAY IN YOUR OWN LANE

Linda A. Feliciano – Chapter Seven — 71
COURAGE TO LISTEN EQUALS INNER STRENGTH

Philip Gustin – Chapter Eight — 83
LEARNING WITH COURAGE

Kari Paramore – Chapter Nine — 93
COURAGE TO TALK TO MYSELF

Tim Yu – Chapter Ten — 105

FINDING SUCCESS BY STEPPING OUTSIDE YOUR COMFORT ZONE

Christina Krag – Chapter Eleven — 115

YOUR COURAGEOUS CHOICES TODAY CREATE YOUR LEGACY

Vera McCoy – Chapter Twelve — 131

FACING CHALLENGES WITH COURAGE

Adam Walker – Chapter Thirteen — 139

COURAGE TO BE YOU!

Carolyn M. Rubin – Chapter Fourteen — 149

DON'T LET FEAR DEFINE YOU

YOU CAN OVERCOME ANYTHING WITH COURAGE

Janet Jackson Pellegrini – Chapter Fifteen — 157

COURAGE

Carmen Ventrucci – Chapter Sixteen — 171

COURAGE TO BE HUMAN

Cesar R. Espino, MBA – Chapter Seventeen — 179

DISCOVER THE COURAGE WITHIN

ABOUT THE AUTHOR — 190

ACKNOWLEDGEMENTS

I am thankful and grateful to each of the authors who have taken the time to share their stories and utilize their life lessons to inspire, empower, and motivate the readers.

I am honored to have each of you in this project, and I want to acknowledge you:

David Selvin
Judy Sweeney
Mike Kroupa
Cortney Vaughn
Duffy Ford
Po Lin Grealy
Linda A Feliciano
Philip Gustin
Kari Paramore
Tim Yu
Christina Krag
Vera McCory
Adam Walker
Carolyn M. Rubin
Janet Jackson Pellegrini
Carmen Ventrucci
Cesar R. Espino, MBA

Thank you so much for your wealth of knowledge and for sharing the obstacles you had to overcome. Your awareness has not only helped you in your own journey but also provided a new perspective to tackle challenges. You are truly an encouragement and inspiration to the readers. **Thank you!**

David Selvin

CHAPTER ONE

ATTRACTING GOOD LIFE THROUGH COURAGEOUS ENDEAVORS

I grew up differently than most people with a story like mine. I actually come from a decent family. My dad was an Optometrist. Growing up as a young boy, he was my idol. I wanted to be just like him. At that time, my mom was a stay-at-home mom who made sure the home was kept up. Life was good then. I would wait to hear the sound of dad's car hit the driveway, and I would run outside like a puppy dog and jump into his arms. My brother was four years my senior. I always wanted to be like him. No matter what he did, I thought he was the coolest guy in the world.

Then, when I was six, my world felt like it turned upside down. My parents split up and got divorced, and that's when things started to get tough. I remember that night clearly. I was waiting by the window for my dad to pull up, but he never came home. Finally watching cartoons, half awake and half asleep, he walked through the front door. He walked into the bedroom, grabbed a suitcase, and walked out. My brother was crying, clutched to his leg, begging him not to go. I remember my mom screaming, telling my brother to stop him. It was a bit confusing at the time, but now I know a lot of my anger and rage come from that day.

One day, we were at the bank, and my mom was crying. I asked, "What's wrong?" And she said, "We only have $3.50 to our name." We were officially broke. We went from living a good life to becoming poor. Kids would make fun of me because of my raggedy clothes and how messed up our house was. This built up a lot of anger, and I felt I could only relate with the local thugs.

I grew up in Los Angeles in the 80s and early 90s. At that time, it was the gang capital. When I was twelve, I started smoking and drinking 40oz of malt liquor and hanging out with some of the local guys in the neighborhood. My mom saw that I was heading down the wrong path, so she sent my brother and me to Boston to reunite and live with our dad. Pops was chill; we could do whatever we wanted, and the streets of Boston became my playground to get into more trouble.

By the time I was thirteen, I had my first arrest and was starting to build a wrap sheet like it was a resume. At fifteen, I was convicted of carjacking. I decided I wanted to be a career criminal. I knew back then that I had the **courage** to change my life, but the only challenge was that I was using it to push myself in the wrong direction! I wanted to be a gangster. That's what I was aspiring to be. To me, at that time in my life, learning that one of the homies got a life sentence was like he was graduating. And the OGs were telling me, "Hey man, you can get away with murder." Because the way the laws were back then, if you're a juvenile under the age of 18 and you get tried as a juvenile, then they can only hold you until you are 18. So because of that, I was getting in all kinds of mess, hurting people, and just doing all the wrong things that would eventually catch up with me in the long run. I never made money in the streets back then. I just like fighting people or hurting people for no reason.

Eventually, I graduated to selling drugs and robbing people to make money. I was hooked on cocaine and drinking every day; the party never stopped. I had met my wife by this time, and we had our first daughter. We lived on our own since we were seventeen. Looking back, I am still not sure why she did not leave. There were times I would not come home for weeks at a time. I was physically, mentally, and emotionally abusive to her. I was burnt out. Living this toxic lifestyle put me in a wheelchair for some time. The year is 2002, and I was picking up guns in North Carolina and bringing them back to Boston to sell them when I got into a crazy car wreck. I had to have four surgeries on my legs. I fell into a deep depression and became eighty pounds overweight.

Fast forward to 2008.... We were living in Oakland, CA. I would always believe everyone owed me something, and now my piss-poor mindset landed us homeless with my wife and now two daughters. My son was not born yet. I remember there were times we had to sleep in our car. I would make a joke and say, "At least we had a Cadillac Fleetwood." It was no laughing matter. And when I had enough money to stay in a motel, we were at the motel on the "ho stroll," where all the pimps and prostitutes would handle their business. It was cheap and what I could afford. This hotel was so bad and notorious that the city of Oakland shut it down. Thinking about these times brings tears to my eyes because I can't believe I was in that bad of a state to let this happen to my family. *Terrible!*

I got sick and tired of being sick and tired. I started to apply for every job that was hiring. I said I'm going straight and not returning to the streets! I applied at Burger King, McDonalds, Walmart, and Wendy's. I was willing to do anything to feed my family. No one would hire me. I eventually got hired at a local barbershop in Deep East Oakland. I always knew how to cut hair. I was good at it and could draw designs, and I credit myself for bringing East Coast razor line-ups to East Oakland. It was a lifesaver. I had $5 to my name and didn't know how to put gas in my car to get the kids to school the day I started. By the end of the day, I had $400 in my pocket, and my family and I were headed to eat Thai food for dinner.

Without courage, faith, and the right mindset, your life will be like a plane on autopilot. If the plane gets knocked off course, the autopilot will bring the plane right back to the course of its journey. So, if you are heading on the wrong course, you TRY to change, yet with the wrong mindset, you are right back on the path of destruction.

While I was working hard, spending sixteen hours a day cutting hair in the barbershop, I saw some of my friends from the street living well. Some of these guys were driving Ferraris and Rolls Royce, and most of them were on private jets. Not to mention, they didn't care about how much a fancy dinner cost. My friend invited me out to a restaurant, and the bill for six of us was $4000, and I was like, wow. I wanted that lifestyle. So the autopilot kicked in, and I was right back on the path of destruction.

I immediately sought out my crime mentors. These guys were doing big numbers in the streets. This was the type of stuff you only saw in the movies. I started making millions, hustling in the street. In a terribly slow week, I still made $40k! My life instantly changed in a matter of months. I would only work three days a week. I took my family shopping every day, and every night, we ate at lavish restaurants, and every month, we took a vacation. I started to buy the cars of my dreams. Life was great. This was hard for me to overcome. I went from homeless to millionaire. We were living in a huge home in a great area to raise kids. How do I stop? It was justified in my mind that this was all I knew how to do. It was the only thing I thought I was good at. This was a hard pill to swallow.

I remember I had a few hundred thousand shipped back to me in the mail, and I went to pick it up from the drop location. I specifically chose this drop because of the way it was located on the street. I could tell when something out of the ordinary wasn't right. I could tell when certain cars or people that did not belong were there. When I went to pick up the money, I noticed some guys standing around who didn't look right. I knew something was wrong. I grabbed the money box, jumped into my ride, and headed home. I immediately noticed three cars following me. On the freeway, I sped off, and they followed me. I cut across four lanes, jumped in front of a semi-rig, cut to the exit, and lost them. I knew at that point something was wrong. The next day, I got a call that my Boston crew was raided. After that, over the course of three months, I lost another $300k between shipments and money (I believe the feds intercepted it). You don't think of jail or death when you are in that moment on top of the world. It's in the back of my head, and I knew it could happen, yet with a scarcity mindset, I thought this was the only way to be rich.

What made me change was my Sun. I call my son Sun because he shines like the Sun that lights up the sky. He has always strived to be like me since he was old enough to walk and talk. Whatever I did, he wanted to do. One day when he was about six, we were driving in my 1964 Impala lowrider, and I watched his every move. If I leaned back in the seat and bopped my head to the music, he did the same. He would stare at me, wait for me to move, almost like he was studying me, and then do exactly what I would do. Then it hit me. I asked myself, "Is what I do and the lifestyle I live okay for my son to do and be when he gets older?" My answer was emphatically NO! At that point, I knew it was time to find a new chapter in my life. This had to be the scariest feeling in my life. I have been shot at, been to jail, car accidents, yet for me to change and walk away from that lifestyle was scarier than all of that. I ask myself why? Because I had no confidence. I was only confident about being a street kingpin because I was good at it. I didn't realize that I was good at it because I did it every day... repetition. I had mentors in the street teaching me who were on a higher level than me. I also had peers who would cheer me on, let me know I could do it, and defy the odds. That is a recipe for success. We were just using this formula to achieve things in an illegal way.

I started asking myself what I could do to allow me to maintain this lifestyle that I could do legitimately. Real estate kept coming back to me as the only answer. I was always fascinated with real estate. I always admired skyscrapers and wanted to get involved in some way, but I did not have the self-esteem or self-confidence to believe I could. Yet the only other people I would meet and cross paths with who had a similar lifestyle were in real estate. So I started to seek out that journey. My past helped me develop that courage in many ways, and I would not change it for anything. When you are in the streets, you have to trick yourself into believing the impossible is possible because when you play at a high level like I was, you make the impossible happen every day. The challenge with most guys in the street is that they think they can't do anything legit. These guys are running a Fortune 500 enterprise that may be illegal and feel they can't run a legitimate business. I remember going to the "clubhouse" (this was where we all congregated and did large business deals amongst bosses) and telling everyone I got a way out. I said, "We can invest in real estate." I showed them the pre-approval and bank statement from the hard money lender, and they told me I was out of my mind and that it was a scam. My family told me to stay away as well. They thought I was up to no good because of my track record. Never take advice on a subject from someone who is not doing better than you. Everyone will always have an opinion. I refused to let that stop me.

My why was too big. I had to do this for my wife and three children. I had to show them there is a better way.

I started searching for the law of attraction on YouTube, which led me to all types of prosperity videos on YouTube. I had to listen to this daily to push myself to the next level. I started filling my mind with books on positive thinking, and I still have to do this every day to avoid going backward. I started to attract the life I wanted. It's one thing to think about the law of attraction... you also have to take action. Action will always beat ambition. I realized my life is a movie I can create, and whatever way I want the ending to be, I can create it.

I followed the same formula I used to rise to the top in the streets: find a mentor, be coachable, do exactly what they say, and act as if success is certain. I met a guy who was local in my area, and he invited me to a party that was full of real estate movers and shakers. I went without question. Being around this new circle of people, being accepted and liked, did something for my self-esteem. That's when I realized I could do anything I put my mind to. I started going to seminars and joining coaching programs and hiring mentors. You don't have to travel the scary road alone. They became my A-Team.

Learn from your past and anything you feel is a mistake. I feel there is no such thing as mistakes, only lessons. Some of my friends who have also changed are ashamed of their past and never want to mention it. They want to leave it buried in the past. Not me. My past made me who I am today. Because of the life I have lived, I can see right through someone's bullshit, and I always stand by my word. My word is my bond! Because of that, it makes me a better businessman and makes it easier for someone to do business with me because they know I'm going to do what I say I am going to do. It has also helped me think outside the box. That is how I started my Credit Repair & Business Funding Company... **Selvin Financial**. I needed to figure out a way to fund my deals. It forced me to learn about fixing my credit and obtaining business credit. After a while, people started asking me for help when they saw my success, so I built a business around it.

I feel that thoughts that flow to you are neither good nor bad. They just are. The perception we put on it determines whether it is good or bad. I considered the line of work I was in for many years good. I would even give thanks to the universe for putting me in that position because it changed my family from being homeless. It was not until I started to view things differently that my perception changed and I viewed it as bad. The greatest certainty is change, and for that reason, you should never be content with being comfortable. That is what hurts most people. They are comfortable and content with the way they live. I had to get uncomfortable to overcome my past life. I like to stay uncomfortable. It means I'm heading to the next level. It means growth. You must be a problem solver.

The biggest challenge is that you have to become who you want to be before you become who you want to be! Scratch your head on that. Some people say fake it until you make it. It cannot become your reality until you become that person and make it your reality. I would tell people I was a real estate investor before I did my first deal. I did not lie and say I did 100 deals when I didn't. The truth is I was a real estate investor... I just did not close my first deal yet. Mindset is everything. You have to have faith, which is like a magic potion, to get what you want. Obstacles will be put in front of you; how you react is how you show and prove your greatness! A hero and a coward both have the emotion of fear. The difference between a hero and a coward is that a hero has the courage to push through their fear, whereas a coward lets their fear conquer them and pushes them back.

What I feel is great is that now all my friends I ran with back in the day are cheering me on and routing for me. I am their Hero! At first, I felt they were in disbelief, and I just kept pushing. I forced them to congratulate me. I refused to give up. One of my mentors once told me you are either growing or dying. What he meant by that is that nothing stays the same. So, if you continue to do the same stuff you've been doing year after year, you are dying. To grow, you have to push yourself constantly to new levels. New challenges. I'm grateful I understand this, and I continue to take my life to the next level. Part of that is pushing through my fears and self-doubt with courage. Knowing I can be anyone I want to be. It's just up to me to be.

Keep Pushing,

David Mr. Prosperity Selvin

About the Author

David Selvin is a testament to the American dream, rising from difficult beginnings as a "Street CEO" to a legitimate business mogul. His turning point came in 2016 when he confronted the realities of bad credit and the dubious origins of his income. Determined to change his trajectory for his family, David began repairing his credit and exploring legitimate business opportunities.

He used a secret strategy involving Business Credit Cards to invest in his first real estate property. Today, David boasts a seven-figure real estate portfolio and multiple thriving enterprises. Through Selvin Financial, he has aided thousands in repairing their credit and securing business funding, significantly impacting lives. His signature Cash Free Real Estate coaching program guides entrepreneurs through savvy real estate investments, teaching them how to build wealth responsibly and effectively.

Social media links:
Instagram: www.instagram.com/mr_prosperity_
Facebook: https://www.facebook.com/davidselvinfinancial
YouTube: https://www.youtube.com/@DavidSelvin
TikTok: @mr_prosperity_
LinkedIn: https://www.linkedin.com/in/mrprosperity

Judy Sweeney

CHAPTER TWO

COURAGE: HAVING FEAR AND DOING IT ANYWAY

I asked several friends what courage meant, and this is the best definition that I got. **Courage** is being afraid and doing it anyway. That's the definition I want you to hang on to as I give you an example.

Preface: This began when I was about twelve years old. At that time, I dreamed vividly. I dreamed in living color, and I did not talk during my sleep. Many times, I would remember my dreams and think they had happened. Example: One morning, I woke up totally recollecting a dream that I had. In my dream, our neighbor called and said he needed my dad to bring his tractor and help him move a cow. This was not an unusual request to call a neighbor if someone needed help with the farm animals or crops. So, I hopped out of bed, slipped on my shoes, and went out the back door. Mom and dad were still at the barn, milking and taking care of the animals.

I stopped at the door because there was cow poop in the barn and called, "Dad."

Dad answered, "Is something wrong?" It was not common for me to go to the barn during morning milking.

I replied, "Jay Stant just called; he needs you to come bring the tractor and help him with a cow."

"They asked me to do what?" I replied, "I do not know; just to help with a cow." So, my dad stopped milking, got the tractor, unhooked the piece of equipment he had ready for that day's work, and headed down the road to our neighbors. When he got there, the neighbor was befuddled and asked why he was there that early.

Dad said, "Judy said you called and needed help with a cow."

He chuckled and said, "I didn't call."

I am sure my dad felt a bit foolish; however, he was so kind he just came back to the house and finished milking the cows. That morning at breakfast, mom and dad realized that I really was having trouble telling dreams and reality apart because my dreams were so vivid. I knew (in my dream) he called. I was not going to concede that he did not call. They devised a plan. If someone calls and I answer the phone, I write the message down before I go back to bed. If there was no note beside the phone, it was a dream. So... if there was NO note by the phone, then NO call, it was a dream.

Now, how does that tie into courage?

One night, I was asleep and dreaming my normal full color, completely detailed dream. In this dream, someone (a big man wearing work boots, cutoff blue jean shorts, and a white t-shirt) entered my room. He thought I was asleep. I actually do not know; maybe he had been watching me sleep. When I moved and saw him (in my dream), and he saw I saw him, he dove underneath my bed. I lay there still for a while, my heart pounding... boom, boom, boom in my chest. Finally, I slithered over where I could peek over the side of my bed. All I could see were two big men's work shoes sticking out from underneath my bed. I started to rationalize that if I stepped out of the bed, he would grab my ankles, and I could not run away. I knew I could not scream; I had never screamed in my sleep. I had not even talked in my sleep; I could not scream.

This is playing over and over in my head. I couldn't step out; he would grab my ankles. I couldn't scream because I didn't scream or even talk during my sleep. After what seemed like many minutes of repeating this in my dream and evaluating the situation further, peeking back over the edge and looking at the big feet, I came to the only conclusion, which was that I must scream. I must scream loud enough that I will wake my mom up. I told myself you only have one screen. I also think you have never screamed in your sleep; you do not know how to scream in your sleep. These two voices were playing back and forth, forth and back over and over in my head, in my dream.

Have you ever had to speak in front of the class, make a phone call or go to the neighbor's house in the dark? Maybe it was just going outside to get something in the dark without a light? Do you remember how scared you felt?

I evaluated the situation: there was somebody under my bed. Those were big feet; it is a full-size grown man. I was terrified, so... in reevaluating again, the only option I had was to screen, and I had to scream loud enough to wake my mother, who was in the next room. Take a deep breath, get ready. I finally mustered up enough strength that I screamed. I screamed as loud as I could scream.

I actually made noise - I screamed, and it was loud enough. My mom woke up and ran into my room to see what was wrong. When she came into my room, I did not know if she called me by name or shook me, but she woke me up. The first thing I remember is sneaking a peak over the edge of the bed, and the feet were gone!

I said sheepishly, "I guess I was dreaming."

She knew I did not talk or scream in my sleep. She had me explain what happened. She looked under the bed to assure me nobody was there. That is a great example of courage. Even though it was happening in my subconscious during my sleep, I had great fear and was doing something I had never done before. Talk or scream in my sleep. To this day, I still do not talk or scream in my sleep, but at that time, in that dream, which was so vivid -- that was my only option. It took courage to make a loud noise to wake my mother. She came running. When we think about courage many times, we have incidences like this, and to us at that time, they may be real or in our imagination. However, it takes real courage to get through them.

It takes great courage to travel through the unknown. Sometimes, it will be a situation with a child. On the first day of school, I had a new class, new friends, and a new family. All of these are times we need courage. "Having fear and doing it anyway."

Something has happened to a child or friend, and we fear for their life. Maybe their life is not in danger, but the consequences of an action or where they are at a given time can greatly impact the future of their life. We look for the courage to be their rock as the unknown unfolds. Has someone been in the wrong place or made a wrong choice, and you are the encourager? You must have the courage to keep painting the picture of overcoming.

We find ourselves terrified about the next step. Can we do it? Are we strong enough? Do we have the skills? Do we have the means to overcome? Can we do it alone? Turn to this verse when you doubt your strength.

*"Be strong and **courage**ous. Do not be afraid or terrified because of them, for the LORD your God goes with you; he will never leave you nor forsake you." ~ Deuteronomy 31:6*

This verse is powerful and speaks on so many levels. First, it is a command to 'be strong and courageous.' Many times, when things are going wrong, or we are in doubt, all we want is somebody to direct us in the right way or come along beside us, saying do this, or do that, this verse does exactly that. It says to be strong and be courageous. It does not say that you should try to be strong and courageous. It is not wishy-washy, wait and see. It tells us how to be. Then, the next part tells us how and why we feel that way. Do not be afraid or terrified because of them. We will talk about who – them - it is referring to a little later, but let us bring it up to today. In our times, what is the challenge that we are facing? Is it being alone, is it falling back into an addiction, is it not being able to say no, is it feeling overwhelmed with financial responsibilities, is it children that have us at our wit's end? Whatever that 'them' is, fall back to this promise. Be strong and courageous; do not be afraid or terrified because of them. WHY? God goes with you, and He will never leave or forsake you. He isn't going to die. He isn't going to divorce you. He isn't going to be sick and leave you alone with all the responsibilities. He isn't going to find someone else who becomes his number one, and he will never leave you nor forsake you…. No qualifications or justifications; just be as strong as the beginning of the verse, and be strong and courageous. What can you be facing today that this does not give you a platform to stand on? Grab this platform and flourish.

Let us go back and look a little bit at the context of this verse. This was the message that God gave to Moses when Moses was 120 years old and was not going to be able to bring the children of Israel into the promised land. In the next verse, he tells Joshua when he summons him. He does this publicly so that everyone hears what he is saying. Let that sink in. Not only did he make the promise to Moses, but he also verbalized it to Joshua. It was not just privately to Joshua, but it was to Joshua in the presence of all Israel. It was the same message, "Be strong and courageous," *and he gave the reason he must accompany them* for you must go with these people into the land that the Lord swore to your ancestors to give them, and you must divide it among them as their inheritance; so, here was his instructions. What he was to do as he went into the land and then continued to say that the Lord himself would go before you and would be with you. Here is another time he is telling him you are not alone; I will be right there with you. How many times can we address our fears if we have somebody with us? It is much easier to stand up to almost any challenge if somebody has our back. God here tells them I have your back and am with you. And then he goes even one further. I will never leave you or forsake you. In other words, I am not going to change my mind and get you halfway there, and then I will decide I do not want to support you anymore. Many others have gone into relationships thinking that the relationship would last forever, and then either you or the other person changed their mind; this is not what God is telling us. He says I will never leave you nor forsake you. You will never be alone (unless you walk away from him), and then he goes right on to say, "Do not be afraid and do not be discouraged." He knows we will have the tendency to be afraid or become discouraged if we have an unknown in front of us. He knows at this time that we will encounter people who will turn around, take another route, and see another shiny object, but he said not me, follow me and I will be there.

⁷ Then Moses summoned Joshua and said to him in the presence of all Israel, "Be strong and courageous, for you must go with this people into the land that the LORD swore to their ancestors to give them, and you must divide it among them as their inheritance. ⁸ The LORD himself goes before you and will be with you; he will never leave you nor forsake you. Do not be afraid; do not be discouraged."

There is a message here for each of us, no matter what we face.

How do I go on after the death of a spouse, a child, or a parent? Do I have the courage to go on after a breakup?

Can I say no to the next drink or hit? Can I begin to make new friends as I start creating a new life?

These are as real as the big feet sticking out from under your bed. It may be we've just been diagnosed with a or someone we're close to with a terminal illness. Maybe we have financial situations looming that there seems to be no out, and what do we do? We must dream up enough courage to overcome the fear anyway. So, today, I want to look at a few more of the definitions of courage.

I started with a friend's definition of courage. Now, I want to bring in another authority on courage.

Matthew 14:27, *"But Jesus immediately said to them: 'Take **courage**! It is I. Do not be afraid.'"*

Even when we see something we cannot explain, "Take **courage**! It is I. Do not be afraid." This was when the disciples saw Jesus walking on the lake; they were terrified. "It's a ghost," they said and cried out in fear. Jesus said, "Take courage! It is I. Do not be afraid."

Acts 27:22 says, *"But now I urge you to keep up your **courage**, because not one of you will be lost; only the ship will be destroyed."* This was Paul's words to the men in the ship.

You Can Overcome Anything! Vol. 13 With Courage | 21

Here are other references to courage or being courageous. You may read them if you choose.

*Acts 4:13, "When they saw the **courage** of Peter and John and realized that they were unschooled, ordinary men, they were astonished, and they took note that these men had been with Jesus."*

*Acts 23:11, "The following night the Lord stood near Paul and said, 'Take **courage**! As you have testified about me in Jerusalem, so you must also testify in Rome.'"*

*Acts 27:22, "But now I urge you to keep up your **courage**, because not one of you will be lost; only the ship will be destroyed."*

*Acts 27:25, "So keep up your **courage**, men, for I have faith in God that it will happen just as he told me."*

*1 Corinthians 16:13, "Be on your guard; stand firm in the faith; be **courage**ous; be strong."*

What is your greatest fear? Is your fear like the feet under my bed? It seems so real; you know it is real. You know you need to have courage and scream because you need someone to turn the light on and say, "See, there is nothing here. You are ok."

Listen, is someone screaming out to you? Do you need to hear their scream and turn on the light?

Darkness is a very real thing. The things that lurk in the darkness are frightening. It takes real courage to scream. The scream may be faint; listen for the screams and be ready to turn on the light. Remember always to be strong and **courage**ous. *"Do not be afraid or terrified, for the LORD your God goes with you; he will never leave you nor forsake you."* ~ <u>Deuteronomy 31:6</u>

We were each created for a purpose. Have you found yours yet? Are you searching for it?

Do you know how to get there?

This is where great courage comes in. Sometimes you must give up who you are to become the person you want to be. Sometimes, you must give up where you are and go where you want to be. Have you ever heard you cannot run to second base and keep your foot on first? You cannot swim in the deep end and still hold onto the ladder in the shallow end. Decide what it is and take a step or scream your message. When fear is too great for you to go along, find that one that will go with you; they will look under the bed, they will never leave you alone, and they will say, **"Have courage, you can overcome."**

About the Author

Judy Sweeney is a Lady of many titles: coach, speaker, daughter, only child, child of God, wife, mom, Grandma, friend, business owner, student, teacher, writer, and reader, to name a few. She values honesty and integrity. She is a problem solver.

Her formal education includes a BS degree in Chemistry and Math from Eastern Kentucky University and a Master's in Public Administration from Kentucky State University.

She worked as a forensic chemist for several years for the KSP lab and taught high school chemistry and math. She is a partner in multiple family businesses. In addition to this, she has pursued real estate investing and various methods to obtain property. She now coaches and speaks on investing in real estate, and she still invests.

She married her college sweetheart while still in college, and they have two boys who are both entrepreneurs. She has two daughters-in-law and four amazing grandchildren. Family is extremely important. She likes most water activities, travel, and being outdoors. She seems to be more of a spectator now as she watches grandchildren play soccer, gymnastics, football, and track.

If you are interested in knowing more about Judy, contact her at:
Judy Sweeney (text) 502-319-4408
Sweeneyjudy01@gmail.com
https://johnnyproperties.com/
Book (available soon): Momma's Real Estate Cookbook

Mike Kroupa

CHAPTER THREE

A LIFELONG JOURNEY OF GROWTH AND DISCOVERY

What is **courage**? Why does it matter? It seems like a word reserved for a major crisis, war, or catastrophe. But courage is something we all need. Courage empowers us to persist in the face of fear and adversity, serving as the driving force that propels us forward during life's most challenging moments.

I've never really thought of myself as courageous. In fact, I know several people who have shown far more courage than I ever will. For example, I have a friend who, accompanied by his wife and young children, bravely escaped from Kabul, Afghanistan, while being relentlessly pursued by the Taliban. The truth is that throughout my life, there were many times when facing a challenge caused me to be gripped by fear. I also like a high level of stability in the core areas of my life. The thought of making a major life change would paralyze me, and I would get stuck — failing to move forward. While it didn't always show on the outside, inwardly, I experienced a lot of anxiety when facing significant changes and challenges.

Fortunately, I found sources of strength that helped me develop the courage I needed to overcome the fears I was facing. As I reflected on this, I was surprised to learn some of the sources of courage over the years. For me, courage wasn't needed to overcome a single large trial, but many smaller challenges were sprinkled throughout life. It all started when I was very young.

I grew up in a small farming community in Michigan. I lived on a farm with my parents for the first five years of my life. Then came the day everything changed. I was five years old. It was a cool fall afternoon; the weather was nice. I was thrilled because my dad had already finished milking the cows and was wrapping up chores. That day, he promised to take me to the cattle auction, which I always loved. I enjoyed sitting beside him in the stands, watching the cows being auctioned off. Mom stayed back at the barn while Dad and I headed home to get ready. I vividly remember watching him settle into his favorite brown chair, starting to take off his muddy boots. But something wasn't right. He didn't finish. At first, I thought he was just messing around, but he didn't respond to anything I said. I was alone with him, feeling confused and scared. I even tried shaking him and shouting for him to wake up, but he never did. That was the day my father died, and I was just five years old.

I don't have a lot of memories of my dad, but the ones I do have are all positive. Let me tell you about just one. I was just starting school about two months before he died. I really wanted a watch to wear, but my mom said I had to learn how to tell time first. Dad, though, he had my back. He told Mom to get me the watch, saying I'd figure it out. It might not seem like a big deal, but it meant a lot to me. Dad had faith in me. He even told others about it. His belief in me boosted my confidence as I tackled school and all the new stuff that came with it. His support early on set me up to face challenges later in life. Knowing he believed in me made me believe in myself.

Years earlier, my parents met while working at a factory. My father and mother dreamed of starting a new life together and having a farm of their own. They eloped and moved from Cleveland, Ohio, to a small town in Michigan to chase that dream. They spent many years building their future together. The day my father died, my mom's life was changed too. She moved us off the farm and into a mobile home about two miles up the road. My mom found work in a stamping plant that made auto parts so she could support us. In many ways, her life came full circle. As a widow, she was single and worked in a factory again. Her dreams of building a life together with the man she loved were gone forever. Money was tight, but Mom found ways to stretch the budget. Every Spring, we would "hunt" morel mushrooms in the wild. Every Fall, we would go into the woods and pick blackberries. We would also grow our own vegetables – tomatoes, radishes, cabbage, cucumbers, and even kohlrabi. She would hand-sew many of the clothes I wore and sew gifts for friends and family. As a child, I just thought she was creative, but now I think she was also doing all this out of necessity.

I have many more memories of my mother, who passed away recently at the remarkable age of over 101 years old—53 years after my father's death. When I reflect on her life, I'm struck by the courage she displayed. She showed bravery when she embraced a new life with my father, leaving behind everything familiar. Yet, her greatest display of courage came after his death, when her life unexpectedly changed course too. Despite facing numerous challenges as a single mother, she persevered, raising me on her own and becoming our sole provider. She instilled in me the value of hard work, such that I always had a job since the day I turned 12 years old. She made sacrifices of both time and money to provide me with a better future, even ensuring I could attend college. Although she lost her dream of a life with my father, I believe she had a silent desire to see me succeed. My mom wasn't big on encouraging words, but her silent example of perseverance through difficult circumstances taught me volumes. Her example taught me that courage often lies in simply persevering during tough times, no matter what life throws your way.

My mom's aspirations for me started to materialize when I went to college. I studied Chemical Engineering at a university nestled in the scenic and remote Keweenaw Peninsula of Michigan. Before college, I had recently embraced Christianity, and during my time at this university, I delved deeper into the teachings of the Bible and the Christian faith. Here, I began to grasp the concept of living a life that honors God. One day, a classmate named Sam demonstrated remarkable courage that left a lasting impression on me. Both of us were studying Chemical Engineering, and we found ourselves in the same English class. The teacher held openly anti-Christian views and was hostile towards believers. Each student was tasked with reciting a poem for the class, and Sam was assigned one that went against his deeply held beliefs. We discussed his dilemma, but I was at a loss as to what he should do. Should Sam refuse to recite the poem and risk failing the class or compromise his values to pass? It was a tough spot to be in, but Sam's resolve to stay true to his beliefs inspired me.

Sam's rendition of the poem was nothing short of remarkable. His choice of tone and inflections brilliantly emphasized the poem's themes of arrogance and pride, turning what could have been a mere recitation into a profound critique. Rather than glorifying the poem, Sam's reading subtly exposed the flaws in its values, portraying them as nothing more than foolishness. What truly stood out, however, was Sam's courage. In a classroom environment where his beliefs were met with hostility, he fearlessly stood his ground, refusing to compromise his principles even at the risk of failing the class. Sam exemplified the essence of character and bravery through his actions, demonstrating that true strength lies in our everyday responses to adversity. Sam's unwavering commitment to his convictions left a lasting impression on me, serving as a vivid reminder that it is during difficult decisions that our character and courage are forged.

Sam and I both graduated on schedule. I ended up working for a Michigan-based specialty chemical company. About a year into my new career, I was married to a wonderful woman. We met at church during my time at university and renewed our connection after graduation. As of this writing, we have been married for 39 years. Some of the things that attracted me to Brenda were her strength of character, compassion for others, and devotion to God. Brenda and I were committed to serving in our local church and working together to help our community. When we were married just under a year, we had the opportunity to put this commitment into practice by helping to start a crisis pregnancy center. This center would exist to offer women in tough circumstances an alternative to abortion and any emotional and practical support needed to follow through on their decisions to give birth. We were offering an alternative to women from a Christian foundation with an emphasis on compassion.

We were blindsided by the level of opposition we encountered when launching this center. While we anticipated challenges from those with differing values, the resistance from individuals who professed to share our beliefs caught us off guard. The process to start this nonprofit organization took over a year. We had to cultivate relationships with donors, develop an organizational framework, implement procedures, and train volunteers. Our procedures and volunteer training were well thought out and of high quality. However, around the time we were preparing to launch, a rival group tried to shut us down. While our stated goals were similar, this group opposed us simply because we were Christian-based. They resorted to underhanded tactics, recruiting from our volunteers, pilfering our training materials, and spreading slanderous rumors. They even succeeded in swaying our newly hired executive director against us, orchestrating a coordinated attack aimed at derailing our progress.

Brenda and I had many sleepless nights while facing this opposition. We felt like giving up – after all, no one was paying us a dime to face all this grief. Two things gave us the ability to persevere. First, we firmly believed that this was a task God gave us. He cared about human life. He cared about the women we would serve. He had gifted Brenda and me with the right combination of skills to help start this organization. It was the right thing to do. We became convinced that God could help us overcome the opposition if God wanted it done. We believed that what we were doing mattered and it was bigger than us. We simply couldn't give up. Our faith in God helped give us courage. Second, we were able to lean on each other for strength. When one of us was at a low point, the other could offer encouragement not to give up. We became a support system for each other. In essence, we could "borrow" courage from the other person when needed. What were the results? Well, the organization we helped to start adapted over time and is still in operation today, over 38 years later, while the rival organization faltered and eventually folded.

The non-profit organization operated smoothly for a while when my company asked me to relocate to another state. This was a big decision we were facing. Having spent my entire life in Michigan until then, I wasn't accustomed to major life changes. But big changes were part of my future. During my 35-year career with the same company, we moved seven times. We moved back between Michigan and Kentucky several times and spent time living in Wales and China.

The move to China was a challenge for us mainly

because it was such a big change. Brenda and I were excited about it because we loved learning about other cultures. What better way to learn about another culture than to live there? On the other hand, we were anxious because we would have to learn to function in a society where we didn't speak the language or know how even simple everyday tasks were done. How would we buy groceries when we couldn't read package labels? (Have you ever put MSG in your coffee because you thought you bought sugar but were wrong? We have.) How would we get around when we couldn't read the maps or figure out bus routes? Although my company gave me a driver to get me to work and home again and get around town, the driver didn't speak English. How would I communicate with him and get where we wanted to go? Somehow, we felt the benefit was great enough to take the risk. We moved to Suzhou, China, and faced these challenges. Fortunately, after we moved, we had colleagues who had lived through many of the same issues. We also had new expatriate friends, some of whom also spoke Chinese. Their support and guidance became invaluable, helping us persist through moments of overwhelming doubt when we contemplated retreating home.

I don't think we were prepared for the feelings of isolation and loneliness we would have while living in Suzhou. This was a much bigger issue for Brenda than me since I was at work all day with lots of responsibility and interactions with others. We had left family behind. We left friends behind. Brenda left a job she enjoyed where she thought she was making an impact. I was commuting to work every day and often worked long hours while Brenda was alone in an apartment. When I had the car, she was essentially stranded. Brenda endured this sense of loneliness for at least two years. While we could make friends in the expatriate community, every year or so, people we were close to would be reassigned elsewhere. This would reignite the sense of isolation. Since she was committed to making things work, she kept searching for ways to connect to the culture and with other people. She eventually found a way to volunteer in a nearby orphanage. She also taught English to children of migrant workers in the area. These activities gave her a sense of purpose. The feelings of loneliness lessened as her relationships grew and deepened. But this took a lot of time, energy, and commitment, and she never gave up.

After spending five years in China, it was time for us to make another move. We headed back to Kentucky, where I continued my work with the same company for another seven years. During this period, retirement started looming on the horizon, and I began contemplating my financial future. While I wished to retire sooner rather than later, concerns about the sustainability of my pension and retirement savings arose. To address this, I entertained the idea of delving into real estate investing to supplement my income during retirement. However, I quickly realized that despite my competence as an engineer, I lacked knowledge in real estate investing. To thrive in this new venture, I would have to acquire a new skill set, effectively embarking on a fresh career path. The prospect was both exciting and overwhelming.

As retirement drew nearer, I delved into the world of house flipping as a potential income stream. It seemed like a promising venture, especially with all the buzz it was generating in the media. Eager to learn, I immersed myself in books, podcasts, and conversations with seasoned investors, absorbing every bit of knowledge I could find. Finally, taking the plunge, I purchased a bank-owned property, a fixer-upper in need of extensive renovations. While contractors handled major tasks like roofing and HVAC installation, my wife, sons, and I rolled up our sleeves for the rest. From revamping hardwood floors to modernizing kitchens and bathrooms and even sprucing up the exterior with landscaping, we poured our sweat and toil into every aspect of the renovation. Despite the modest profit margin at the end, the experience proved invaluable. It demonstrated my ability to navigate the intricate process of buying, renovating, and selling a property. Moreover, it ignited a newfound passion for real estate investing, bolstering my confidence to pursue this avenue further.

When this first project was nearing completion, I started looking for another one. I was the kind of person who would normally keep my plans to myself. I worked up the courage and told everyone at work what I was doing and that I was looking for a house that needed work. A colleague told me about her neighbor Gary, who needed to sell his house, and it really needed a lot of work. I had been reading about how to talk directly to sellers, and now was the time to put that into practice. I then did one of the hardest things I had ever done: knock on Gary's door. He opened the door, and we talked for a while. We talked about his struggles and his plans. We talked about the house and what it needed. In the end, I agreed to buy Gary's house, and he was able to move on. This turned out to be a huge project, and I still had a lot to learn, but when completed, I felt much more comfortable using real estate to build supplemental income. At that point, I started to look for a date to retire.

After deciding to retire, I focused on learning real estate investing inside out. Attending classes, conferences, and networking events was awkward at first. I felt insignificant compared to the successful investors I met. However, when I found the nerve to start asking questions, many were willing to help and give advice. I committed to applying what I learned. Gradually, my skills improved, and I became more comfortable as an investor. Now, I have a strong foundation in real estate that supports our financial future, with our investments growing yearly. I've also realized the diverse opportunities in real estate and stay dedicated to learning and finding new investment paths. Whenever I get too comfortable, I know it's time to find the courage to challenge myself further. While I might never need to show exceptional courage like some people I know, I still want to see my courage grow through the challenges I face.

Brenda and I have encountered some big personal hurdles in recent years. Approximately four years ago, Brenda received the diagnosis of Parkinson's disease, a formidable challenge. More recently, we were blindsided by another unexpected blow when she was diagnosed with breast cancer. As I write these words, Brenda is preparing for surgery, less than a week away. The uncertainty of the outcome looms, but she draws strength from her unwavering faith in God, a source of courage that has sustained her through various trials. Over the years, she has witnessed the steadfastness of God in her life, which gives her confidence moving forward.

What insights have I gained about courage along my

journey? I've come to see courage as something you build over time rather than a fixed trait. It's something you nurture and develop. When others believe in you, it fuels your courage, empowering you to confidently tackle new challenges. Courage isn't just about facing the big trials; it's also about persevering through unexpected hardships, like losing a loved one. It's about sticking to your principles, even when it's tough. Courage often emerges strongest during tough decisions and opposition, finding strength in faith and the support of those closest to you. Keeping your eyes on meaningful goals can fuel your courage when the going gets tough. And perhaps most importantly, I've learned that courage is something you can cultivate and grow through practice. So, let's embrace courage and chase after our dreams.

About the Author

Mike Kroupa brings over three decades of experience from his career at a multinational corporation, specializing in project management, problem-solving, and leadership. He and his wife, Brenda, have lived in various locations, including Michigan, Kentucky, Europe, and Asia. Mike and Brenda actively served their church and community in every place they lived.

In 2016, Mike and Brenda embarked on a new journey in the realm of Real Estate, driven by their passion for enhancing their community. They find immense fulfillment in acquiring properties directly from sellers, employing innovative solutions to address their needs. Mike has over 500 hours of real estate training, is an active member of his local Real Estate Investor Association, and is continually expanding his expertise.

Website: www.BlueGemKY.com
Facebook: https://www.facebook.com/bluegemky
Email: Mike@BlueGemKY.com

Cortney Vaughn

CHAPTER FOUR

FROM DESPAIR TO DESTINY

COURAGE, FORGIVENESS, AND FREEDOM COVERS IT ALL

Have you ever pondered the boundaries of your life, those limits that seem to hold you back? They were not there by accident. They are there for a reason. We often push past them, reaching for what we desire. However, what if I told you that it is not our strength that propels us forward but a divine intervention? Divine intervention is believing that a higher power, such as God, can intervene in and change events. That is the inspiring journey I want to embark on with you: Personal growth and transformation guided by a higher power.

~DAMAGE IS FAST, AND HEALING IS SLOW~

Life often resembles a broken road strewn with obstacles and challenges that can easily let our fears obstruct us. But he will lead us through when we learn to confront those fears with **courage** in our faith in God. Many mistakenly believe that bravery and courage are synonymous, using them interchangeably. However, while both describe acts of heroism, they are not identical. Bravery is the nonexistence of fear, while courage takes a step forward despite it. This courage will be your guiding light on this journey of personal growth and transformation. Some argue that courage takes more strength because it means sharing your story even though you may be ridiculed, rejected, and misunderstood. Have you ever considered the profound impact of reacting out of hurt, whether from others or within yourself? If the answer were as simple as that, how would we truly comprehend the depth of our 'very well mind?' These questions ignited my Curiosity as I embarked on the next chapter of my personal growth journey. Right now, the first thought that comes to mind is, where do I start? Right? That is how most people today respond. The list of never-ending thoughts begins.

One of the most courageous choices you can make is to release what has or is hurting your heart and soul. In my last chapter, *"From Despair to Destiny, "Love Covers it all,"* I talked briefly about how I grew up and the challenges I faced in my childhood. When you grow up in a childhood out of adoption, many people do not understand that the obstacles continue into your adult life. You could grow up with the absolute best family who adopts you, but the emotions, feelings, and generational curses still bleed into your life.

I grew up in a beautiful home with incredible opportunities and experiences. Yet, a puzzle piece was always missing: a connection to my biological roots. That missing piece fueled my courage to explore my identity, embrace my story, and find strength in being both adopted and loved. Knowing that my birth parents faced a problematic loss so I could have a chance at a better life fostered empathy within me. I realized that everyone has their own struggles and reasons for their choices. This understanding shaped my compassion toward others. I am grateful for the gift of empathy, which reflects God's love within me. This empathy - the ability to understand and share the feelings of others - allows me to connect with others on a deeper level. It fosters love and compassion, essential for personal growth and transformation, as they help us understand and accept others and ourselves.

~HEALING TAKES TIME; BREATHING IN THE SIGH OF SURENDER~

Surender is crucial in our personal growth journey. It is about letting go of our need for control and accepting that healing is a process that takes time. It is about acknowledging our limitations and trusting a higher power to guide us. One of the most meaningful themes in scripture is the confirmation of God's safekeeping. In our everyday lives and in times of trouble, the Bible invites us to embark on the love God offers the world. The verses of the book of Psalms give powerful and spiritual reflections on the character of God and our relationship with God. When the world is against us, we remember God's infinite grace is for us. The Bible is our most incredible resource, a reminder that we can find refuge in God. The book of Psalms is mostly about worship and the trials and triumphs of a life in pursuit of God.

Just as the sky filters out toxic substances, God can distract harmful ideas and fears from our thoughts. He scatters the fiery attacks of the enemy. On this side of heaven, we will never realize the full extent of His protection. Setbacks are a natural part of life. We stumble, we fall, but the key lies in rising again. Each delay is a chance to learn, grow, and refine our approach. The refusal to surrender, even in the face of repeated disappointments, reflects the indomitable spirit of humanity. Embrace the healing process, which is the key to personal growth and transformation. *"When you appreciate what you have, I conclude that you conclude the importance of everything I have lost to lead me there."*

Healing began with acknowledging the wounds that come with adoption. The invisible scars etched into my soul. I recognized that adoption was not just about gaining a family; it was also about navigating the complexities of identity, feelings of abandonment, and unresolved Trauma. I grappled with questions about my identity. Who was I? Where did I come from? These uncertainties can create a sense of disconnection. I felt the ache of separation, the longing for answers, and the occasional sense of not fitting in. Adoption can evoke feelings of abandonment. It stirs emotions of loss and rejection. Adoption often involves Trauma, separation from your birth parents, adjusting to new surroundings, going through the motions of foster care, and adapting to a different family. These experiences can leave lasting emotional imprints.

~HEALING IS HARD; THERE ARE LOTS OF ARROWS BUT ONLY ONE TARGET~

You dare to show up even when we cannot control the outcome. What is courage without uncertainty, risk, and emotional exposure? There is no courage without vulnerability. "The myth of Vulnerability:" "Vulnerability is weakness." "I don't do vulnerability." It is easier to create pain than to identify pain. "I can do it alone." There is always suffering without connection, love, and belonging. You cannot do it alone. You cannot predict doubt and discomfort out of vulnerability. "Trust comes before vulnerability." Vulnerability boundaries are not vulnerability. "Vulnerability is disclosure." "You do not weight vulnerability by the amount of disclosure." "You determine it by the amount of it by the amount of courage to show up and be noticed when you cannot control the outcome."

In the Bible, Psalm 91, often called the *"Psalm of Protection,"* says, *"He will cover you with his feathers, and under his wings, you will find refuge; his faithfulness will be your shield and rampart."* This imagery portrays God's protective care, like a mother bird sheltering chicks under her wings. It speaks of safety and security. *"You will not fear the terror of night, nor the arrow that flies by day, nor the pestilence that stalks in the darkness, nor the plague that destroys at midday. A thousand may fall at your side, ten thousand at your right hand, but it will not come near you."* Even amid chaos or danger, God's shield surrounds you. You will only observe with your eyes and see the punishment of the wicked. If you say, *"The Lord is my refuge." "You make the Highest your dwelling; no harm will overtake you, and no disaster will come near your tent. He will command his angels concerning you to guard you in all your ways; They will lift you in their hands so that you will not strike your foot against a stone. You will tread on the lion and the cobra and trample the great lion and the serpent."* Victory over adversity. You will overcome challenges. *"Because he loves me,"* says the Lord, *"I will rescue him; I will protect him, for he acknowledges my name."* God's love leads to rescue and protection. Acknowledging God brings blessings. *"He will call on me, and I will answer him; I will be with him in trouble, deliver him, and honor him." "With a long life, I will satisfy him and show him my salvation."* This imagery is the assurance of a fulfilling life and ultimate salvation. The psalmists assure us that God's safekeeping endures forever; in our moments of strength and weakness, God watches over us. These psalm Bible verses help direct us back to God in times of struggle and encourage us to give thanks for our blessings.

(2 Corinthians 10:1) "The weapons we fight with are not the weapons of the world." On the contrary, they have the divine power to demolish strongholds. We demolish arguments and every pretension that sets itself up against the knowledge of God, and we take captive every thought to make it obedient to Christ. In this verse, the apostle Paul writes: *"By the humility and gentleness of Christ, I appeal to you, I, Paul, who am 'timid' when face to face with you, but 'bold' toward you when away!"* Paul emphasizes the contrast between his demeanor in person ("timid") and his shamelessness in his letters or when absent from the Corinthians. His authority comes from Christ, and he seeks to demolish arguments and pretensions that oppose the knowledge of God. This verse reminds us that our spiritual

weapons are not physical but have divine power. We engage in a battle of ideas, seeking to bring every thought into obedience to Christ. It encourages us to approach challenges humbly, relying on Christ's strength. The Curiosity of my adoption led me to explore my roots. I researched my biological information and history, my birthplace, traced family trees, and pieced together fragments of my past. Each discovery, whether a faded photograph or a forgotten memory, contributed to my healing. Forgiveness was not about condoning past actions but about freeing myself from resentment. I forgave my birth parents for their problematic decisions and embraced compassion. Letting go of the expectations I told myself I had to measure up to, allowed me to accept my unique narrative without bitterness.

My adoptive family and I built and established new traditions, religious beliefs, a blend of cultures, celebrations, and shared moments. These new traditions replaced any voids left by unanswered questions and became part of my healing tapestry. I learned to be gentle with myself. Healing was not direct; it had its twists and setbacks. When grief resurfaced unexpectedly, I reminded myself that healing was not a race. It was a lifelong journey, a sigh of relief. My adoption story became a source of purpose as I had almost lost my sense of purpose from the pain of discovering the unknown after 30 years. My deepest pain is what cultivates my greatest compassion, and is not compassion the one thing that drives us in love? I started advocating for adoption awareness and shared my experiences. Helping others navigate their healing process gave meaning to my struggles. I moved beyond the label of "adopted." Instead, I embraced the label of "resilient" and "loved." My identity expanded to include both my biological heritage and the love that enveloped me and shaped my personal motherhood journey. Resilience emerged from facing my trauma head-on. My healing journey became a testament to courage.

~HEALING TAKES COURAGE, A GUIDING LIGHT OF HOPE~

If God has put you in a position, it is for a purpose. He meets us where we are and in small ways. *"With a whisper, like the butterfly, saying, Find me here. Home is here, where I am. The butterfly, a symbol of transformation and change, reminds us that personal growth is a gradual process in small steps, just like the butterfly's metamorphosis from a caterpillar to a beautiful creature."* It is a journey of transformation, just like ours.

Healing will ask more of you. More rest. More self-love. More letting go. More time for learning. More space for transformation. More honesty about how you feel. More time developing good habits. More courage to try new practices. More time cultivating your inner peace. More faith in God, yourself, and the process. Healing was not about erasing pain; it was about transforming it. I found gratitude for the intricate threads that wove my life together. I was grateful for the courage of my birth parents, the love and differences of my adoptive family, and the resilience that defined me. I feel rewarded because I have gotten through many things in my life that typically destroy the lives of others. In the end, adoption taught me that healing was not about erasing scars; it was about weaving them into a beautiful mosaic, a testament to love, courage, and the human spirit. Love and compassion are the best antidote to fear. Without fear, we would never recognize the vulnerability within ourselves and others that gives us the courage to face our fears.

A transformed mind sees the world through a different lens, aligned with God's will and guided by His love and wisdom. It is a mind open to change, growth, and transformation. An outstanding summary of the poem *"Try Again" By W.E. Hickson* admits that when we try to achieve any targets, we may fail once or twice, but we should not surrender. It is against the dignity of man. ***"Try Again" by W.E. Hickson*** beautifully captures the essence of resilience and determination. When faced with adversity, it's easy to feel defeated, but hope whispers to us, urging us to persevere. When the world says give up, Hope whispers, *"Try it once more."* That gentle yet powerful force encourages us to take that extra step and attempt again. It defies defeat, defies resignation, and fuels our determination. (*Psalms 139:14*). *"I praise you because I am fearfully and wonderfully made. Your work is wonderful. I know that full well."* From Despair to Destiny, "Courage, Forgiveness, and Freedom Covers It All."

Cortney Vaughn

About the Author

Cortney Vaughn, the author of this novel, has a diverse range of interests and experiences. Born in Las Vegas, Nevada, she now resides in Minnesota. Her writing journey began in 2021, and this novel marks her second contribution to the *"You Can Overcome Anything"* series. Her previous work was published in *"You Can Overcome Anything with Awareness."* The title of her last novel, *"From Despair to Destiny, Love Covers It All,"* suggests themes of hope, transformation, awareness, and love.

Beyond writing, Cortney enjoys spending time with her children, fishing, learning to play the guitar, and exploring unfamiliar places and opportunities. Her passion for storytelling shines through her work, and readers can expect a heartfelt and engaging narrative in her latest novel.

Email: despairtodestiny@gmail.com
www.linktree.com/despairtodestiny

Duffy Ford

CHAPTER FIVE

CREATING A GREAT LIFE WITH COURAGEOUS SMALL STEPS

I've never really thought of myself as courageous. I've not served our country, I've never stopped an armed robbery, or done anything overly spectacular that exhibited a considerable act of bravery. But my wonderful wife, Paula, and I have built an amazing life that took many calculated risks to accomplish. And sometimes, it takes **courage** to take those risks.

I was born in Louisville, Kentucky. My parents, my older

sister Cinda, and I moved to Richmond, KY, when I was four. It was a small college town with a population of under 20,000 about 100 miles east of Louisville. My oldest sister, Linda, who was already married, stayed in Louisville. We bought an average brick ranch on nine acres about 10-15 minutes from town. A few kids were in the neighborhood to play with, and it was a good place to grow up.

My parents - especially my dad - were very strict about grades. I think my dad would admit that he was a prototypical football jock in high school. He goofed off a bit and probably just skated by. After high school, he had a rift with his parents and moved to California, where he eventually met my mom. Dad went to college a little later in life. I believe he was in his early to mid-twenties when he started. He worked his way through college and got excellent grades while studying accounting. He passed his CPA exam on his first try, which I believe is very rare. Dad stressed education very much. My mom and dad eventually got married and moved back to dad's hometown of Louisville.

My mom grew up in the Bronx, NY. She moved to California with her first husband. He was never really talked about, but I believe he had some mental issues and they divorced leaving her essentially a single mom with two young girls, and I'm not sure what happened to him. My mom had some units - I believe an eight plex - in California that I would hear about several times. My dad thought it would be best to sell them before moving. We usually watched the evening news during dinner. Every time there was a story about real estate on the news, my mom would comment that those units would have been worth a fortune if they had kept them. I believe the first time I heard her mention a dollar amount it was $800,000.

Several years later, that amount was over a million dollars. That was a huge sum of money to a young, middle-class boy growing up in the 70s and 80s. My mom often told me how smart I was, how I could be anything I wanted and to shoot for the stars.

My dad and I were huge University of Louisville basketball fans. We would travel from Richmond to Louisville and back for sixteen to twenty basketball games a year. That was our thing. During the late 70s and early 80s, I became a Boston Red Sox fan and Wade Boggs was my favorite player. I was a stats nerd and would keep tables of stats for Boggs and all the Louisville basketball players. Way before the internet was even a thought, dad started bringing me the USA Today newspaper to get stats from the box scores. One day, the headline "90% of Self-Made Millionaires Come from Real Estate" caught my eye. I don't remember much from the article except that it seemed like buying real estate was a pretty easy way to become a millionaire. This article plus mom's talk of the units planted the seed that eventually caused me to get into real estate.

My dad was the poor dad from Robert Kiyosaki's Rich Dad Poor Dad. We weren't poor, and I grew up middle class, but his mindset was like that of Kiyosaki's poor dad. Go to school, get good grades, get a good job, and that's life. My parents divorced when I was a junior in college and my dad moved back to Louisville. He eventually remarried but developed prostate cancer shortly after and died following a five-year battle at sixty-three. My dad was very smart but, was admittedly, not good with his money. He died with a five- or six-year-old Saturn car and not much of anything else. About a month before he passed, he told me that he had an insurance policy that would pay the condo off for his wife and that he had nothing to leave me except a $12,000 insurance policy. He told me that he had pissed away all his money on cars and the latest gadgets and made me promise not to do that. He was sad and embarrassed about this and told me that it was a sin and that he had nothing more than this with the amount of money he had made over the course of his life. I assured him I didn't need anything and that it was okay, but I could tell it bothered him. I did not want to be having this conversation with my son on my deathbed.

My mom's post-marrying story was long, and I could probably write a chapter just on her journey, so I'll try to keep it short. Mom did not attend college but was a very sharp lady. She stayed at home with me until I started elementary school. She started working at a print shop, and sometime around my 8TH or 9TH grade years, she became a receptionist at Sherwin Williams factory in Richmond. She probably worked there for thirteen to fifteen years, and eventually, she moved back to Louisville and got a condo near the house I had with my first wife. She would pick our son Nicholas up after school and watch him until one of us could pick him up. It was very nice... until it wasn't. Mom developed Alzheimer's disease and went downhill quickly. I eventually had to become her legal and financial guardian and move her into an assisted living facility. This was a very stressful ordeal, and it caused me to have a minor, stress-induced heart attack. I recovered quickly, with no lasting effects, and two weeks of sick time allowed me to get her stuff in order. Most of her money was eaten away by the assisted living facility costs, but I was amazed that she had amassed a nest egg worth about $140,000 (2006 dollars) despite probably making 10% of what my dad made. I often think my parents would have been worth millions if my dad had let her manage the finances.

School came very easily to me, and I got A's, B's and an occasional C with minimal effort. This irked my dad, and he would constantly get on me to do better. He eventually started grounding me if I got C's. I could get four A's, a B, and one C, and I would get grounded for two weeks. I would be so mad during the two weeks seeing my friends, who made worse grades outside playing. This caused me to dislike school, but it did eventually cause me to do better. I would usually find a way to bring the C in the class that I cared nothing about to a B. I was good at math and science, so I always heard that I should be an accountant or an engineer. My dad was an accountant, and that seemed boring, so I chose engineering.

My dad wanted me to attend Notre Dame or the Air Force Academy, but I was set on returning to Louisville to attend school. I was accepted into the University of Louisville's Speed Scientific School because of my 3.5ish high school and my whopping 23 or 24 on the ACT. I took it early in my junior year, hung over after a night of pounding beers with high school buddies. Underage drinking is BAD! I probably could have gotten a 27 to 30 had I retaken it with a straight head and any effort to study. There is no telling how much scholarship money I left on the table.

Most of my college was paid for with money my parents had saved, Pell Grants, and student loans that I took out - unbeknownst to my parents - that I used for CDs, food, clothes, and beer. I skated by my first two years with about a 2.3ish GPA, but after a subpar 1.67 summer semester GPA topped off with a D in Geography of US and Canada, my dad jumped my @$$. They would not continue paying for me to hang out, party, and goof off at school. I straightened up a little, took later classes, and limited my partying to weekends. I found that if I just went to class, paid a little attention, and did the assigned work, I could get A's and B's pretty easily. I pulled my undergrad GPA close to a 3.0 and believe I had a 3.7 or 3.8 in my master's classes. Dad was happy....

My first wife, Angela, and I met in college, and we had our son Nicholas right as I was finishing my master's classes. I had already graduated with a bachelor's degree in civil engineering and took a job at a local engineering firm, Presnell Associates. We bought a house because I didn't want to continue throwing away rent money, and we married shortly after. I did drainage design in our transportation department while I finished my master's thesis. I quickly became bored with that and made it known that I wanted to be involved with all aspects of roadway design. I quickly caught on and became a lead project engineer on several projects. Angela and I started investing in our 401K's, and I was asked to become a company shareholder at the young age of 28. We were living what I call the poor dad dream.

Angela and I started having issues shortly after getting married. We trudged along, were doing okay financially, and had a seemingly good life from the outside looking in. But inside, things weren't that good, and she was not happy. We stayed together, sold our first house for about a $10,000 profit after only a few years, and built a nice house in a nice suburban neighborhood. The issues of two careers, raising a son, and just doing life were too much for us. At the time, things seemed fine to me, but looking back, I realize we were both fairly miserable. We trudged through the week and lived to party on the weekend, but we did manage to stay married for fifteen years.

Sometime in about 2003, my mom started talking about what a burden her condo would be to us "kids" if something were to happen to her and she would like to sell it and rent something. Looking at her finances, she could not afford to rent even a modest apartment in a decent area for what she wanted to spend. Angela and I eventually asked if she would like us to buy it and rent it to her for a break-even - or small loss - per month. She thought that was great, which we did in early 2004. When we went to do the financing, we used a fellow college engineer buddy, Drew Schaefer, who had turned into a mortgage broker, to get us a loan. I expressed interest in getting more heavily involved in real estate. He mentioned our local REIA group KREIA (Kentuckiana Real Estate Investors Association), and gave me their website information, which I quickly checked out. Another college friend, Jay Long, was vice president, and I mentioned it to Drew. Drew said that Jay was the F-ing master, that he had done many deals, and that I should connect with him.

I had only seen Jay once in the ten years post-college, but I dug out the phone book, looked up Jay's number, and called and left him a message. I didn't hear back and tried again about three weeks later. As I left him a message, he picked up and we talked briefly and set up lunch. At lunch, he complimented me for doing something but then - in Jay fashion - told me a few things I could have done better: buying below market value, renting for $300/month cash flow, and not doing business with family. He was 100% correct on all three. He also suggested that I read Fast Cash with Quick Turn Real Estate by Ron LeGrand. I think I bought it that day or the next and read it within a few days. I was amazed at the many ways you could make money with real estate – wholesaling, fix and flips, rentals, lease options! I called Jay back, and we had lunch a week or two later. I asked him if it was that easy. Jay said, "It's simple, but it's not easy," meaning that the process was a simple task but took time and effort, most of which people just didn't do. Jay recommended coming to and joining KREIA, which I did.

At the time, KREIA was held at a local restaurant between my office downtown and our house. During the first meeting, I walked in, and I was mortified! There were hundreds of people there. For an engineer, who would just as soon be left in a corner by himself to do his work, it was a daunting task to walk through the door. There's a bad joke – how do you tell an introvert engineer from an extrovert engineer? An introvert engineer looks at his shoes when he talks to you, and an extrovert engineer looks at your shoes. I made my way to the bar, bought a drink, and managed to talk to a few people. Luckily, I saw Jay, and he introduced me to a few people. Some of the first few people I met were Cliff Hayden, Jamie Greenwell, Rod Owens, Joe Burnett, Joe Burnett Jr., Harry Borders, and Mike Butler. Jay, Cliff, Jamie, and all the rest became some of my best friends, and we would later bounce deals off each other. Harry became an invaluable team member as my trusted attorney. There are way too many to mention, but I met some of the most helpful, genuine, great people at KREIA.

After several calls pestering Jay while simultaneously looking at several junker houses a week during lunch, I began to submit offers. It was so scary submitting those offers. After about twenty or thirty rejections, I finally got a cash offer of $12,500 accepted on 2804 Narragansett. Talk about being terrified! I had discussed the process with the wifey but to come home and tell her that I got an offer accepted and that we would have to use a home equity line of credit (HELOC) to buy the house if I couldn't find a buyer before the closing. If I recall correctly, her only words were, "I hope this works!" I called Jay, and he was super excited. He came, and we drove to check out my first "deal." Jay said, "It was a pretty good deal, but I would have probably paid $8-10,000." I did not find a buyer before closing and had to purchase the house using HELOC funds. That was a scary check to write!!! Not long after closing on the house, I found an old landlord to purchase it for $15,000. After closing, I made about $2,300. A few months later, I made another deal and made over $4,000. Both deals probably took 5-6 hours, so I was hooked at $1,000/hour! Over the next five or six years, I did twenty total deals. Most were wholesale deals with a few partner rehab deals with Cliff Hayden. Despite a few losses, my profit for those twenty deals was about $95,000. I spent some money on mileage, meals, cell phones, education, and networking events but mostly stockpiled the cash in a business account.

From 2005 to 2009, my mom's health deteriorated quickly. Nicholas was hitting teenage years and having some behavioral issues, and my marriage was getting unbearably bad. We had to sell "mom's" condo and move her into an assisted living facility a short time later, and I had my health scare. Things were getting miserable at home. In March of 2009, after fifteen years, we mutually decided to divorce. Although the marriage was bad, it was still tough to walk away, especially with a soon-to-be 16-year-old, a paid-for house, and a net worth approaching $900,000. I was scared for my son, I was scared financially, and I was scared that as a quirky, bald engineer, I would not be able to find anyone else. I feel bad saying this, but the divorce was the best thing that ever happened to me. I was immediately much happier, and my confidence soared. And I think that Angela would agree that we are both in a much better place.

On the real estate side, Cliff and I had a flip deal, stagnating on the market in 2009 during the aftermath of the housing crisis. I had a lot of cash in the deal, and Cliff agreed to let me have it for what we had in it to keep as a rental. My ex-wife never wanted rentals due to the "hassles" of tenants. Several months later, Cliff found a deal that he wholesaled to me, which would become my second rental. I quickly learned the power of leverage, property appreciation, positive cash flow, the tax benefits of depreciation, and a wonderful thing called cash-out refinance. I put nearly $14,000 in the bank when I got permanent financing on my second rental. I also got a very good tax refund due to all the rental property write-offs. I was hooked again – this time on rentals. Over the next several years, I would add two to four rentals per year to my portfolio. I put approximately $30,000 and $18,000 in the bank for my third and fourth rental acquisitions after doing cash-out refinances. So much for needing money to buy real estate!

I was very happy single, but in March of 2012, my world forever changed for the better. Friends dragged me to a party at our mutual friend Tim Wessel's house. I met his sister, a beautiful six-foot blonde named Paula, who was recently divorced. There was an immediate connection, but I was too aloof to realize it for several hours. Throughout the day, we all had a great time, and I realized that aside from being beautiful, she was smart and very funny too. We parted ways after a fun day. I hoped to see her again but wondered if she would really be interested in a 5'9" quirky guy. To my knowledge, I don't think I had ever met a taller woman who had any interest. I was afraid of rejection but told my friends that I was interested and would love to see her again. A few weeks later, I went with friends to watch Louisville basketball play for a birth in the Final Four. Paula showed up, and again, we had a connection. Thankfully, Louisville won, so she didn't see what a baby I could be after a loss. We had our official first date about a week later, and luckily for me, we have been together pretty much ever since.

We started spending a whole lot of time together, and once we got serious, we alternated houses. Despite some very severe neck issues on my part, about fifteen months after meeting, she decided to sell her house and move into mine. After she sold her house, Paula had about $110,000 to invest and asked me what I would recommend. I showed her typical stock market returns, private lender returns, and a few variations of different rental portfolio options, including one like mine. I showed her how I took my $95,000 and rolled it into ten or twelve rentals and how her portfolio could be worth over $1.5 million in fifteen years. She liked that option and trusted me to make it work for her while she focused on a demanding job. I don't know if I would have had the courage to allow someone I met fifteen months prior to do this. A few years later, we sold my house, and I made a good profit. We took that money and some cash from Paula and bought a fixer-upper a few miles away for $248,000. We put about $80,000 into the property, made it our own, lived there for about eight years, and sold it for $523,000. We rolled that profit into our dream home, which we built on a two-acre lakefront lot. A huge plus for all these personal home sales is that the profits are tax-free if you've lived there for two years.

In 2016, while still suffering from severe neck pain, I scaled down my engineering job to four days a week to focus on my health and to work more on our real estate business. Paula and I were married in a private ceremony on the Eiffel Tower during our second European river cruise. In October 2020, I mostly retired from my engineering job and now focus 90-95% of my time on our real estate business. It enabled me to help with our house build as a GC for most of the inside work and to renovate an 8-plex with some partners. Last year, Paula was able to scale back to 24 hours per week at her job. Despite all this scaling back at work, our net worth increased 10x what many people make in a year. I don't say this to brag but to pound home how wise, calculated financial decisions can yield unbelievable results to some. Personally, I feel like the luckiest man on the planet. I am married to Paula, a beautiful woman inside and out. She is smart, funny, loving, caring, and an amazing decorator and detailed planner. She -unlike me- is a people person. We have tons in common, but she also complements me perfectly in areas where I struggle. I thank God every day for bringing her into my life and for the life we have.

I am in no way, shape, or form a hero. That title is reserved for true heroes like our military, police, firefighters, and first responders. But Paula and I have made some calculated and sometimes courageous decisions that have allowed us to live an amazing life. Buying my mom's condo as a rental property took some courage. It took some courage to walk into my first REIA meeting and network, buy my first flip property, and partner with Cliff on some rehab properties. It took some courage to buy more rentals and incur debt. It took courage to leave a bad marriage and pursue a six-foot blond who many would think was out of my league. It took courage for Paula to leave a bad marriage and sell her house fifteen months after meeting me. It took courage for her to let me lead her down the rental property path and for both of us to scale back from our well-paying jobs.

I will leave you all with a few final pieces of advice. Be grateful for what you have and have a true, well-thought-out vision for your life that will pull you forward. Develop a plan to get you to that vision. Lastly, have the courage to make the decisions and to take the steps to follow your plan to reach your vision.

About the Author

Duffy Ford is a professional civil engineer with thirty years of experience in roadway design. He worked his entire engineering career at Qk4, Inc. (formerly Presnell Associates, Inc.). He semi-retired from there in 2020 as a Senior Project Engineer/Project Manager/Co-Owner and still does some occasional consulting for them. He began doing real estate on the side in 2004 and did twenty wholesale and rehab deals in five years before starting to acquire rental properties in 2009. Duffy has been involved in approximately a hundred real estate deals in some capacity. He and his wife Paula have been together for twelve years (married for five) and have a portfolio of rental properties. They enjoy traveling, sports, and concerts and recently built their dream lake home together. Duffy has an adult son, Nicholas, from a previous marriage. He is still actively involved in real estate. He does wholesales, rehabs, lease options, rentals, and short-term rentals, and he has a passion for learning, growing, and helping others.

Facebook: www.facebook.com/duffy.ford
Instagram: https://www.instagram.com/duffyfordrei/

Po Lin Grealy

CHAPTER SIX

STAY IN YOUR OWN LANE

What thought came to your mind when you saw the title of this chapter? You may have thought I was going to talk about driving. I would like you to consider that our thoughts and beliefs are like lanes in our brains. A lane is a thought. In the lane, what are you thinking about and paying attention to? Let me give you an example. You are in a coffee shop and have your laptop in front of you while working on a project. The ideas are flowing, and you're enjoying your cup of coffee. As you sip your coffee, you look up and notice a lady with brilliant pink hair standing in line waiting to order. You might think wow, that looks fantastic; I wish I could wear my hair like that, and now your mind begins to remember a time when you dyed your hair orange and received a lot of feedback, some good and some not so good. Next thing you know, your mind is thinking, I'm so glad I'm sitting here drinking my coffee because I don't have to get up and wash the cup when I finish. And then you begin to think about your kitchen, and it's been a long time since the cupboard handles were last changed; it's been a long time since they were upgraded. The next thing you know, your focus has completely diminished, and your flow of ideas for the project you were working on has stopped. You are now thinking about the handles on the kitchen cabinets. How many have let their mind wander off like that? There are a few components in this above example.

1. The distraction
2. Comparison
3. The loss of momentum

Let's go back to the idea that our thoughts are lanes. If we want to stay focused on a thought or an idea of where we are going, we will want to put tools in place to help us stay focused by giving our thoughts and our minds some rules. We can call these boundaries. Let's look up the Oxford Dictionary description of a boundary. https://www.oxfordlearnersdictionaries.com/ a line that marks the limits of an area; a dividing line; a limit of a subject or sphere of activity.

If we look at this meaning, we are saying that we are

giving our thoughts a line that marks the limits of an area dividing line. This could indicate that I will not allow my mind to go past the limits I have decided to adhere to while working on this project. When this boundary is implemented, the result is more productivity, more focus, and more satisfaction with a project or goal that has been accomplished.

I invite you to apply this definition of a boundary, 'staying in your lane,' to your interactions in relationships with others and your thoughts. Remember the definition of a boundary as a line that marks the limits of an area. Can you think back to a time when you were having a conversation with someone, or they came into your emotional space or your physical space without asking for your permission?

How did you feel? How did you react? In the context of staying in your own lane, did you find it necessary to set up an emotional or physical line that they cannot step over? Was there a consequence? Did you decide to stop seeing them or spend less time with them? These are ways of expressing staying in your own lane. This is where you are only concerned about the area you stay in, your lane, thoughts, and focus. These boundaries can also be applied to your own thoughts. When you think about a boundary as being a border or a limit, I suggest that you think of putting a limit or a border around what you think and see. These are internal boundaries.

Your mind and body might protest when you first start implementing these new boundaries. These protests may present as a headache, an internal pressure that screams this is too hard, and this is too painful. Let's return to the idea that our thoughts and behaviors are a lane. A lane is now being created through the boundaries you are saying, such as no more smoking, no more gossiping, no more comparing, and no more victim thinking. As you continue to create new thoughts, you are creating a new lane. Through repetition, the brain will understand and be able to help you navigate these new thoughts. In the beginning, though, your brain will resist, but as you continue to chop down old thoughts, rip up old lanes, rip up roots, the root \ of these thoughts, new lanes are being created. When you are consistent in making new thoughts, you will begin to create new habits that now become a new behavior.

May I reflect on a time when I was learning about staying in my own lane and setting up a boundary for myself? Every time I fly, I always seem to have my flight either delayed or canceled. I was always anxious about flying and I never really understood why. As I began to ask myself, what is this pattern of flights being canceled or delayed? I would be traveling with others to a conference or with friends, and we would have different flights. Their flight would go as planned, but my flight was most times either delayed or canceled.

Now I have had a lot of introspective times and seasons of doing inner healing and inner child work. Anyone who does this kind of self-reflection or work to heal our past can know that inner healing is a process. You may have dealt with certain things, but as you have more understanding, sometimes deeper awareness can begin to take place. For me, I did some investigating and inner searching and realized that indeed, this was an Inner child, a young child wound that became a fear—a fear of flying. Let's begin with when I was a little girl. A Canadian family chose me to come with ten other little girls and four social workers to fly across the Pacific Ocean from Hong

Kong, China, to Vancouver, BC, Canada. This destination would now be my forever home. Each of the other little girls was also flying to their forever homes. I didn't choose this; I was a child. Decisions were made for me.

Wow, this could be a really exciting adventure in a different land and country. As a three-year-old girl, though, this was pretty scary. Now, please understand that adoption is truly a wonderful thing. Children are given a chance and opportunity to experience life in a way that they probably never could, given the circumstances that they may have come from. I am very grateful for the home that I was given. I had a very loving family and a very happy childhood. My childhood experiences were very happy and loving. I am giving my experience from a three-year-old perspective. These are some of the thoughts that I had as a young three-year-old child. Why was I leaving my homeland? Had I done something wrong? All these thoughts were swirling in my mind. At that moment, I had said to myself, I am not going to fly and planes will be delayed so I don't have to fly. Flying is scary.

Pretty powerful statement when you think about it, right? Think back to what may have happened to you as a child, and you may have said something similar, "I'm not letting that happen again." It wasn't until I had actually gone back to that day as a three-year-old that I had somehow made that promise to myself. Fast forward to my adult days, and literally, all planes I have booked have been canceled or delayed. Imagine I'm an adult, and I have done a lot of my inner work, realizing that I made this vow to myself as a child. This brings me to recently when I got on a plane. It was a short flight, a flight that was maybe three hours long. I was headed to a conference from Victoria, BC, Canada, to Las Vegas, Nevada, US, and I found myself having the beginnings of a panic attack. I felt everything inside me screaming, "Stop the plane; I need to get off," but I mustered up enough **courage** to say to myself, "Hey, little Po, remember I decided to go on this flight; I decided to fly together, this was my choice. This plane ride is going to be an adventure. When I get to Las Vegas, Nevada, I will have new and fun experiences and meet and connect with new people. This is my choice." Would you believe that my flight home, back to Victoria, was on time? It wasn't delayed, and it didn't get canceled. I've since flown to Denver, Colorado, and It wasn't delayed or canceled either! Amazing.

I have noticed that the more I focus on what is good and where I want to go, even if things are bad, when I know that things happen for me to learn and to grow, this definitely gives me the courage to continue on the path that I am choosing for myself, which I believe in the long run is a good path for Humanity. When I keep showing up and doing the things I am completely terrified to do, this gives me confidence and more courage to continue staying in my lane and going where I know to go, to follow my inner compass. In time, you will reflect and notice the things and thoughts of jealousy and comparison. Things that you thought were very scary turn out not to be.

With persistence and repetition of guarding your thoughts and staying in your own lane, you gain the courage to do more things that terrify you. You will realize that your reactions will be much less than they were, and you won't entertain those ideas anymore. You will see that you get to choose your thoughts, your behaviors, and even your habits. There is more physical and mental peace when you stay in your own lane. The drive and momentum to stay focused on where you want to go become more consistent, and you easily see when those roots (jealousy, comparison, fear, and anxiety) start. You can chop them down right away and continue on your path of freedom and choice. You will notice the distraction, you will notice if you are being pulled and micro-managed, and you can choose to say no and carry on. You are able to observe it instead of diving deep into it. You are able to remain detached from it. Staying consistent with this practice gives you the courage to keep you in your own lane. The things that you are reaching for become realities, little by little, bit by bit. Guilt fades away, joy is more consistent, and peace is more consistent. Love is more consistent toward yourself and others. Congratulations on discovering that you can stay in your own lane!!!

About the Author

Po Lin Grealy is passionate about seeing people reach their potential. She has spent thirty years in a traditional medical institution as a caregiver to older adults and then the administrative experience of preparing people for surgical procedures. After her own experience in the medical system, recovering from a life-changing accident, Po Lin found inner peace in working with the medical system and adding the energy and breathwork component. She decided to help others on their health journey by learning about the power of energy and that our body can heal itself. Po Lin now helps many people become healthy. She uses her thirty years of medical knowledge in anatomy to help others maintain a healthy body, mind, and emotions. Through energy and breathwork, headaches are gone, blood pressure is lowered, mood is changed, and internal peace is restored. She integrates breathwork and learning to scientifically help solve anxiety and blood pressure problems and improve blood chemistry.

Instagram: www.instagram.com/po.6540
Email: tembracingtouch@gmail.com
Newsletter through SOV: spiritofvictoria.com

Linda A. Feliciano

CHAPTER SEVEN

COURAGE TO LISTEN EQUALS INNER STRENGTH

As I sit and ponder on the phrase "you can overcome anything," I can't help but think about the many times I believed that I simply wouldn't make it out of this situation. You see, at a very young age, I learned that not everyone who "loves" you and wants to "protect" you is actually doing it in your best interest. There are people who, for reasons unbeknownst to the average person, are intent on taking advantage of or hurting those weaker. This fact holds true in every aspect of life, from the animals out in the wild to world-renowned CEOs. Some call this survival of the fittest. Charles Darwin stated, "It is not the strongest of the species that survives, nor the most intelligent but the most responsive to change." Growing up in Chicago gave me many opportunities to "bob and weave" while walking to school or simply playing in my backyard. By the time I was twenty-five, I had endured over fifteen years of domestic violence, not realizing that this was not the "norm" and that life could really be different for someone like me. I had no clue about the many opportunities available to me, nor could I imagine that it would be possible to become a bestselling author and highly sought-after tax strategist, all while raising three wonderful children on my own in Florida. For the most part, I did not believe I would live past thirty years. But there was something inside of me that screamed, don't you quit!

On January 18, 1994, I was on my way to a black tie and red carpet affair that included local dignitaries. I was in the last trimester of my third pregnancy, and in my opinion, I looked like the goodyear blimp covered in satin and lace with a navy evening gown. Nonetheless, I proceeded to my destination to make an appearance and slip out the door before anyone noticed I was gone. Needless to say, the universe had different intentions for me on this day. To add insult to injury, instead of wearing my normal wool coat, I decided to wear the light winter jacket to be more comfortable since the gown already had multiple layers and my belly was huge. As I warmed up the car, yes, in the Midwest, it was necessary to start the car and let the engine run before driving out of the garage because the overnight temperatures tended to drop below zero, causing the engine oil to thicken. Well, wouldn't you know that this particular day is historically known as one of the coldest days in Chicago? In the morning, the temperature was a whopping 21 degrees below zero; by the time I was heading out, it was barely 11 degrees below zero.

On my way to the venue, light snow started to fall, but I thought nothing of it. This time of year, this was normal. I completely forgot that when the temperature drops below zero, the road becomes icy, and if the sidewalks have not been plowed, they will form a thin layer of ice that makes walking at a normal pace difficult. When I arrived at the location and parked my car, I proceeded to get out and started briskly to walk toward the door through the snow. The event would begin in the next 7 minutes, and mine would be the third presentation of the evening.

Suddenly, I felt like the red carpet was pulled out right from under me, and I flopped to the ground. Here I was, dawning the most beautiful pregnancy gala gown, and now I was on the floor covered with dirty snow and freezing. You would think I'd be embarrassed, but when I looked around and saw no one, I sat there and laughed through the tears that flowed from yet another failed attempt on my behalf to "do something right." How was it possible that I, today of all days, was unable to walk gracefully from my car and into the ballroom? Was I so clumsy or inept at walking gracefully? My mind was flooded with memories of many failed attempts at succeeding and all of the naysayers' discouraging words. Oh my! What a sight! I know my belly was as big as a house, and I was not a petite woman by any stretch. I chuckle at my many attempts to get up and continue to slide and fall. There was nothing to grab on to, no one was outside, the event had started, and now I was not just fashionably late; my attire screamed of everything except beauty and poise.

After what seemed like an hour of sitting on the floor,

crying and laughing, I heard someone call my name. Apparently, my presentation would start in five minutes, but someone realized I had not yet arrived. The team began to check outside to see if I was pulling into the parking lot when someone spotted me on the ground. Little did they know that I had been there contemplating whether or not to make a snow angel. You see, with all the adversities I had already faced in my life, I learned that at times one must simply grin and bear it until something else comes along. Within a few minutes, two handsome strangers in tuxedos lifted me off the ground, and now I was embarrassed. After assuring them I was fine and did not need an ambulance, I begged them to let me in the side door so I could go to the ladies' room and try to salvage my appearance before entering the ballroom. Grudgingly, they obliged.

Once inside the ladies' room, I wiped my tears, corrected my makeup, and dried my dress as best as possible with the hand dryers. Then, I heard my mom's voice, "Julie, oh my God! Are you okay? What happened?" And behind her, I heard another voice say, "Oh, this is your daughter? She's beautiful!" Something about that woman's voice filled me with peace and the **courage** to finish freshening up my appearance so I could work up the nerve to enter the ballroom. Little did I know that this woman, Stella, was about to become my most prolific and stout supporter.

While my mom began to go down her list of I told you so (I told you to come with me, I told you not to come alone, I told you to leave early), she used her condescending tone to remind me that I was a mess now, my dress was dirty, my makeup was running, and what's worse I may have injured my baby by refusing an ambulance. In my head, this simply meant she didn't want me to dishonor her by being or looking imperfect. All the while, the lady with her hugged me, assured me everything would be okay, and started helping me get myself back together. She knew I still had a presentation to make and reassured me it would be spectacular.

As the evening went on, I found myself pondering the words this newfound stranger spoke to me while I was disheveled. Was it possible that even after all I had just experienced, I could deliver my presentation without a hitch? Would I get up in front of a room full of dignitaries and forget that I was in complete disarray just moments ago? The thought that a few simple words would give me the courage to get up, smile, and keep going was mind-boggling at the moment. Regardless, I proceeded to give my presentation. Guess what? I got a standing ovation, and yes, everything was all right.

At this moment, you may be thinking that this is insignificant and that giving a presentation is no big deal; however, this is just the beginning of the many hurdles I didn't know I would have to overcome. Thanks to this woman's encouraging words and unwavering support, the next five years of my life would change so drastically. Stella is also responsible for helping me become the woman I am today. We were officially introduced after my presentation during a brief intermission. That moment for me was magical. It was as though I had been wandering through this forest called life, alone and without a friend or a loved one to show me the way to civilization. When we were formally introduced, I could look at her face to face, and as we both looked down, we noticed that we were in the same pair of shoes, except in different colors. This little detail further strengthened my desire to want to know how this woman could be so kind and supportive to a stranger.

I wanted to understand how someone who apparently had it all together was wearing the same shoes I had on. I mean, after all, I had to use a coupon to get mine, and she clearly was from high society. After we saw our shoes, we spent about five minutes laughing and decided we would meet at a later date to discuss so many peculiar details of this evening.

For the next couple of weeks, Stella would call me and invite me to dinner, and every time she called, she'd say to me, "Remember, you are a beautiful, intelligent woman, and there's nothing you cannot accomplish. I believe in you, and you are not alone." She did not know that when we got off the phone, I would spend at least twenty minutes sobbing and the rest of the day wondering what it was about me that caused her to say those things. On February 9, I gave birth to my beautiful daughter. When she was placed on my chest, the look in her eyes further assured me that my life had to change. This wonderful little girl deserves her mother to be the woman that Stella described.

As time passed, Stella became my surrogate mother, best friend, mentor, and adviser. One day, she approached me and said, "I have noticed that you cover up your body, and I want you to know I know what is going on. You may not trust me a hundred percent yet, but I want you to know that I am here for you and that whatever you have been told in the past is not true. You are a beautiful, intelligent woman capable of many things and you do not deserve anything less than the best; no one should be hurting you because you don't deserve that either." My eyes welled up with tears and I could not hold back any longer. I had my first breakdown and cried for what seemed like hours as she hugged me and assured me it was okay to cry and let go.

Fast forward five years, and I managed to not only get away from that horrible situation, but I was successful at obtaining my divorce, permanent order of protection, and sole care custody and control of my children while representing my case before the Illinois Family Court Pro-Se. Yes, that's right! I, the person who believed she would amount to nothing and was an idiot, was able to research the laws and statutory cases and present evidence and facts of the case without the assistance of an attorney, and I won! Thank the living Lord! I know He definitely helped. But I also had Stella by my side to encourage me not to give up and not to give in. Once I was free, I had to pick up the pieces of my life and move forward with the promises I had made to my children in silence and on paper. This would be no easy task.

One of the promises I made was that although our history was one of abuse and brokenness, we would overcome all obstacles and negative statistics attributed to abused women raising children in a large city like Chicago. Stella continued to be there for my family and me for the next twenty years. She always encouraged us to do more, be better, pursue our dreams, etc., even pushing me to go back to school and obtain my degree, pursue my dream of home ownership, and start my own business and nonprofit to help others.

In 2008, the nation experienced the worst economic downturn since the Great Depression, and naturally, I was a casualty of this event and lost my full-time job. What was I going to do now? My oldest was in college and I still had two in high school, plus I was supporting my mother as well. Stella, whose health was beginning to fail, said, "Now it's time for you to launch out on your own and start that business; I know you can do it." Can you imagine? My retirement account barely had $5,000.00, and my savings account was holding only $750.00. How was I supposed to start a business? Oh, did I mention I was also in college trying to complete my bachelor's?

There, I was about to embark on one of the many senior projects, which was to construct a business plan. Guess what I decided to do? Yes, that's right. I used the words Stella had so often spoken to me and used this project as a catapult for the business I would start one day.

By May 2009, I had aced my senior project with the business plan and met with some local SBA counselors and attorneys to review and critique my work. To my surprise, everyone was supportive and welcomed the business ideas included in those pages. I had one more thing to do, and that was to determine what the overhead expenses would be, get funding, and commence.

While seeking out office spaces and locations, I stumbled upon a landlord who had many properties that were vacated due to the recession. At this point, my only source of income came from unemployment, $550.00 per month, so I was desperate for an opportunity. I am unsure if that desperation was written all over my face or if this kind soul saw the same thing Stella saw in me because after showing me several locations, he asked to meet for coffee to discuss further.

I knew that I was only doing some basic research and had no real intention of renting a local space then, but I proceeded to meet with him. As soon as he sat down, he said, "I know you liked this last office we saw. Why aren't you pulling the trigger and taking the space?" I had no choice but to tell him the truth that this was part of a business plan school project for a business that I would one day own.

The following words out of his mouth, coupled with his actions, significantly changed the trajectory of my life. He looked at me and said, "Julie, I believe in you; I know that you can do whatever you set your mind to do. Therefore, here are the keys to the place. I will see you in three months, and at that time, you will have the first month's rent and the deposit to secure the location. Feel free to customize it as you want, and we will sign the lease documents in three months." My jaw dropped to the ground, and my eyes welled up with tears; here I was again in front of a stranger who saw something in me that those close to me would not see or acknowledge.

Rather than refusing to accept the key and his proposition, I humbly reached for the key and thanked him profusely for believing in my dream. Wouldn't you know that in less than ninety days, I somehow had everything I needed and was able to lease the building? Never once was I unable to meet my monthly obligations at the office or home during my tenure at this location.

Today, it has been fourteen years since I first found the courage to launch out on my own and start this business. During this time, I have learned to value myself and give my clients the best services I can offer without fear. I used my Business Administration and Accounting degree to help others launch and grow their businesses. I use strategies that have been tried throughout the years and have proven successful for many. I have also pursued other revenue streams and have put systems in place that enable me to educate others on stewardship and wealth strategies. My love for dissecting the legal system and almost by circumstance have made me an exceptional tax and wealth strategist. As an Enrolled Agent appointed by the United

States Department of the Treasury for the IRS, I have a 98% success rate in cases I have handled that have been much to my clients' satisfaction.

Stella left earth approximately ten years ago, but I still hear her encouraging words, and I continue to pursue my dreams. Five years ago, I started a nonprofit that enables me to give back to the community and help others who have been victimized to become CEOs of their lives and businesses if that is their dream. The key to achieving anything you desire is simply not to quit. One of my favorite poems is Don't Quit. Although there is some controversy about who the author is, the words within continue to remind me that in life, one simply must not quit. Sometimes things will go wrong, and yes, there will be twists and turns, but if you don't give up and smile while you are going through them, you will find you have succeeded beyond your wildest expectations. You might be the next Stella in somebody's life, so go for it; you can do anything!

About the Author

Linda A. Feliciano EA, was born in Chicago, IL, to a wonderful couple who taught her that in life,

you've got to go after what you want and never give up. She's the mother of three, grandmother of one, and most importantly, a Minister of the Gospel of Jesus Christ. Being the first of four children, growing up in the city of Chicago, and a survivor of domestic violence, she has overcome many obstacles and today is a successful entrepreneur.

Linda is a keynote speaker and has been featured on several national radio shows. She is the founder of a small business management consulting firm and a full-service tax practice and accounting consultancy firm. She has helped thousands of small businesses save millions of dollars. Her mission is to teach stewardship in finances, health, and Spirit to the glory of God.

Her desire to help survivors of Domestic Violence and Child Abuse overcome statistics has caused her to launch her most recent endeavor, Asher Ministries International - a 501(c)3 Not For Profit Corporation with programs to educate and empower underserved communities to launch businesses and live purposeful lives. Linda is now working on bringing awareness to the importance of submitting yourself to the Lord and presenting your body as a living sacrifice so that God can continue to be glorified here on earth. Stay tuned for this next episode; it will change your life.

www.asherbusinessgroup.com
www.facebook.com/taxninjasuperstar
www.linkedin.com/company/asherbiz
www.facebook.com/AsherBiz

Philip Gustin

CHAPTER EIGHT

LEARNING WITH COURAGE

Leaping for the grass-covered bank, I watch over my shoulder as the old farm tractor tips into the dry creek bed. Dumb-founded and pulse-pounding, I stare in disbelief. I cannot believe it. Yet there it is on its side in the dry creek bed. Except for the drive here, I have owned this tractor for all of ten minutes. I look around to see if anyone saw me, then laugh nervously, knowing no one is around for miles. At least I am not hurt, double-checking myself. Yep, still in one piece. With a couple of deep breaths, my pulse slows a bit.

Moments ago, I thought, "How hard is it to drive a tractor?" Inexperience and ignorance failed to consider several things when I attempted to answer that question. My ten minutes of experience have taught me something, though. When the tractor is leaning acutely to one side, like next to a creek bed, raising the bucket arm to full height will make the tractor top heavy and put it at risk of tipping over.

My bruised ego tries to explain itself. It is compelled to recount the events even though no one is here. I indulge it because, quite frankly, I want to hear this explanation myself. "Lifting the bucket was not my intention," I begin. All these levers are a mystery to me. When I got on the tractor, I was eager to try them out and see what they do. Experimentation was in order. Reverse. OK. Forward, yes, that makes sense. With the tractor rolling along, I continued experimenting with the levers. And there it is—my first mistake: distracted driving. Half-watching where I'm going, I tilt the bucket. Raise the bucket arm. Lower the brush hog. Raise the brush hog. Power the brush hog on. Then off. Two-wheel drive. Four-wheel drive. Suddenly, the tractor lurches to the right. I look up in a panic, stomping on every pedal, hoping to hit a brake. Thankfully, the tractor abruptly stops.

Sweat breaks out on my flushed forehead, realizing how close I am to the edge of the creek bed. I survey my situation. The bucket arm is still raised from a previous "experiment" in this precarious position, which cannot be good. I should lower it, but which lever does that? With a trepidatious gamble, I pull one. The bucket tilts. Nope, not that one. I pull another. The bucket arm moves. Oh no! I see the bucket arm rise upward. Time immediately slows down. Unfolding in front of my eyes, the consequences of that mistake start to become clear. The bucket arm goes up, and the tractor starts to tip. I feel the blood drain from my face as my mind races to figure out if I can save it. Then fear grips me as I realize it is going over, and there is no stopping it. I need to save myself! I leap uphill for life and limb.

Standing on the bank, I look around at the rolling green contours, the stark contrasting red barns, and the faded and flaking yellow saltbox farmhouse with blue trim. A former horse ranch sits between the junction of two creeks and behind a large bluff with an expansive view in the direction of the small country town several miles away. There is a cave on the backside of the property, once the home site of the infamous Dalton gang, who used these natural features to evade law enforcement. It is a rundown ranch now. I bought it in a cliché and familiar attempt to escape corporate America and my life as a software engineer. I want to be outdoors and work with my hands, away from my computer monitor. It is peaceful and fresh here despite the poorly maintained house. The sing-song of the birds. The rustle of leaves in the breeze. The babble of the creek. I can breathe here. Deer grazing in the late evening. To look up and see actual stars fill the unobstructed night sky as the milky way cuts a pathway to the wonders of the universe. The neighbors are few and far between. Still, they are friendly and look out for each other. This is a long way from the life I've known.

I am looking back at the red tractor lying on its side. What am I going to do now? I am 80 miles from home with no tools or equipment—no ropes or chains in sight. It was only supposed to take a minute to unload my new purchase and return home. I cannot just leave the bloody thing here. Maybe there is something useful left in these old barns.

In the barns, I see a lot of rusted, old junk. Most of it is just garbage. Ah, ha! This might work. A 10-foot steel cable. It is not ideal. I do not see anything better. Surely, I can make this work for my predicament. Ten feet is not very long, though, and I'll have to get my truck relatively close to the tractor. If I drive it down around this large creek-side tree, I may get close enough to tow the tractor upright. Between the stiffness of the cable and the need for maximum reach, I tie a simple crisscross knot. It is the only thing I can figure out to do. One end around the tractor axle and the other end to the hitch of the truck. Alright. Here we go.

The frogs and the locusts are buzzing louder now, drawing my attention to the sinking sun and the dwindling daylight. Maybe this will work. Put the truck in drive and slowly ease off the brake. I feel the tug of the tractor. It starts to move as I gently press the gas pedal. Slowly the tractor sits upright. Nice! This could have gone a lot worse... wait. What the...? I put my palm to my forehead—great googly moogly.

The knot I tied in the steel cable is now too tight to untie with my bare hands. My only mode of transportation is now tightly tied to an anchor the size of a tractor. In a dry creek bed. In the middle of nowhere. At sunset. This situation just went from bad to worse. Once more, I head to the old barns for a solution. In moments like this, when I feel like a fool and proven incompetent, I am most baffled by the sentiments of friends and family.

"I can't think of a time you weren't **courage**ous," my sister once commented. It is a sentiment shared by several friends and family. It was strange to hear as it is not a view I hold about myself. I know of many times I was less than courageous. Obviously, acting with **courage** rarely feels like it looks. Why is that? If this is courage, then for me, it often feels like a foolish mistake. I have since come to know that this is the feeling of learning. It is one reason why learning often takes courage. Courage can be the willingness to feel foolish to learn new things and gain new skills. This challenge becomes more pronounced as we age. It involves stepping out of one's comfort zone, facing challenges, and persevering in the face of fear and uncertainty. It is natural and expected to perform poorly, make mistakes, and possibly look foolish while learning. Yet, at times, we resist anything that brings those feelings out, and learning often does that.

Maya Angelou once said, *"Courage is the most important of all the virtues because without courage, you can't practice any other virtue consistently."* The willingness to consistently engage in the learning process is the courage my circle of family and friends attribute to me. A software engineer could be considered a professional learner. The ongoing pursuit of knowledge is the key to adapting to new technologies and staying relevant in the workforce. It requires consistent and deliberate learning. As a result, I have pursued learning from my first programming job until now, and it has spilled over into every area of my life and interests. And I have often played the fool and the incompetent. Though that doesn't get easier, there is always a benefit to learning, even if the benefit is intangible at first. Sometimes, what we learn only serves as a lesson on what not to do. Knowing what not to do is as important as knowing what to do. Still, learning adds to our life story. We keep growing, and life stays interesting and exciting.

Unfortunately, I have seen over time that as people age, less and less are willing to face and submit to the learning process. To feel incompetent for a season of learning. For some, deliberate learning ends when they leave school. Some after they get a "good enough" job. For some, it's pride in life or fear of failure. People use many reasons to prevent themselves from pursuing new interests and learning experiences. Albert Einstein famously remarked, *"Once you stop learning, you start dying,"* expressing the importance of continuous learning in our journey.

We all have varied interests and proclivities. Certain things that, old or new, draw our attention. Some of which we have let go. Sometimes, we cannot explain why we like completely unrelated interests. Yet those interests are part of who we are. Our combination of interests is one thing that makes us unique and unlike others in this world. We are obligated to pursue our interests and bring our uniqueness into this world.

When we stop growing, we can find our life stagnating and boring. Is this you? Have you ever felt stuck? That you haven't reached your potential? Or directionless? Or just bored with your life? Have you reached the end of one role in life? Mustering the courage to learn something new enriches every aspect of our lives, regardless of age. A biblical proverb says, *"The one who gets wisdom loves life; the one who cherishes understanding will soon prosper."* ~ Proverbs 19:8 NIV

The intersection of courage and continuous learning is where transformation occurs. Courage empowers us to confront our fears, take risks, and pursue our dreams with determination. By fostering a sense of curiosity and wonder, learning encourages us to explore new ideas, perspectives, and cultures, leading to greater personal fulfillment and a deeper appreciation for the world around us. Learning with courage will take us to our next passion, level, and story. *"Life is either a daring adventure or nothing at all."* ~ *Helen Keller.*

"Courage lives within us, even when we don't feel brave," a Harvard Business Review study notes. The study concluded that courage is a teachable, life-enriching skill that is different from a flash of bravery that one may summon in an anxious moment. That means courage can be learned and developed. That is exciting. We should know that courage is a skill, too, and that it improves our lives. Exercising continuous learning is one way we can practice and develop courage. Together, they form a powerful synergy—a dynamic interplay between the courage to confront our fears and the curiosity to pursue new knowledge and experiences.

Courage is not just about facing our fears head-on; it is about recognizing and pushing past our vulnerabilities. It's about acknowledging our limitations and embracing them as opportunities for growth. This notion underscores the vulnerability inherent in courage and continuous learning—the willingness to embrace uncertainty and take risks, even in the face of potential failure or rejection. Through this vulnerability, we cultivate resilience and deepen our capacity for growth.

Mastering one skill naturally leads to the need to know and learn another. This is skill stacking. Skill stacking is such an important concept. The more skills we have, the better our value. The better our value, the better our lives. By adopting the skill stacking approach, we can create a unique value proposition that sets us apart in the job market and opens new opportunities for growth and development. It all begins with the courage to learn new things. We must continue to walk the path before us and follow our interests to new places. And maybe when you find yourself facing a fear at a critical time, you will stand up and face it with courage.

Public speaking is considered one of the biggest fears of most people. I was among them. Jerry Seinfeld joked about a study that said people fear speaking in front of a crowd more than death. If true, it means the average person attending a funeral "would rather be in the casket than doing the eulogy." As funny as that may be, when my own father passed away and I was asked to speak at the funeral, I immediately felt fear and panic about speaking in front of so many people. My dad was well-loved, and there would be a large crowd attending. How could I not honor this man who means so much and all those coming to pay respects? It was one of those once-in-a-lifetime moments when I had to rise to the occasion or regret it. Sitting with this feeling for a bit, though, it started to feel familiar. I was practiced at facing this. My life of humbly submitting myself to the learning process had inadvertently given me the courage to draw on and stand and speak at a critical time for my family.

Now, heading back to the barns, I feel the daylight fading, and I need to get this knot untied and have my truck detached from this tractor soon. My search finds half a pair of pliers and a metal rod that I can use like a hammer. I commence pounding the "plier" into the knot to loosen it. After fifteen or twenty minutes of targeted and aggressive pounding, I am finally able to free the knot. Alas, the truck is free, and the tractor is upright. I park the tractor in the barn.

As the sun sets and the stars begin to twinkle overhead, I find myself lost in contemplation, pondering how courage and continuous learning intersect in our lives.

It's a complex and multifaceted relationship that defies easy explanation but is nevertheless essential to our growth and development as individuals. As I stand beneath the vast expanse of the night sky, I'm filled with a profound sense of gratitude—for the opportunities I've been given, the lessons I've learned, and the people who have supported me along the way. For it is through their encouragement and guidance that I've found the courage to embrace the unknown and the curiosity to continue learning, one step at a time.

Today, the ranch is a gathering place for family celebrations, an endless supply of entertaining learning stories, a cherished memory of working with my father, and I now know how to operate a tractor safely.

About the Author

Philip Gustin is a member of a large, loving family and a seasoned software engineer with a rich portfolio of contributions to prominent companies like Pluto TV, Paramount Global, Pop TV, TV Guide, and the Williams Company. His expertise spans the development of intricate data delivery systems, electronic program guides, and user-friendly video streaming apps, notably enhancing viewer experiences for flagship shows such as the critically acclaimed "Schitt's Creek." At Pluto TV, Philip is instrumental in revamping frontend applications, focusing on creating shareable components and processes leveraging cross-platform technologies. He is deeply committed to personal growth, embodying the values of continuous learning and fostering a growth mindset within his team and beyond.

LinkedIn: https://www.linkedin.com/in/philip-gustin/
Email: philip@gustin.life

Kari Paramore

CHAPTER NINE

COURAGE TO TALK TO MYSELF

My personality has always been the type to see in others what I've never seen in myself. I LOVE to talk to people and encourage them to become what I see in them by helping them see it in themselves. Don't ask me to see value in myself! It has always been forbidden in the back of my mind. Seeing value would be selfish and too proud. To put yourself up on a pedestal would only mean that God would bring you back down from where you just put yourself. You know that whole

"Pride comes before a fall" thing?

I always thought: Don't have friends who feel valued and proud of themselves and help you improve because that's just going to make you "stuck up." I don't know where I got this thought from, except for being my worst critic. I've always considered myself a bad thing and that there was always someone better, not realizing that you are for someone else out there. Someone needs your values, strengths, and weaknesses. They need your highs and your lows, and that is why I'm writing this chapter.

Where am I going with the value and pride thing? I've always been the skinny one growing up, and still then, I had big hips, big lips, and the biggest mouth. It was considered a "not such a good" thing. There was always something to work on with my body. All I saw in my house as a young kid and carried into my marriage were the magazines "First" or "Lose Weight," or "How to Lose 10 pounds in 10 days," etc.

I'm not blaming anyone or anything but myself for allowing what others think and their lack of self-esteem because they didn't know or were not taught any better. We must allow others in our lives to help bring us up, to help make us shine, and to help accept ourselves so we can go forward to the highly confident person whether we are skinny, fat, short, tall, black, white, yellow, green, man or woman, or in this day, whatever you call yourselves.

I'm sure there are many self-help books on this subject, but I've not read them because Kari did not want to face the truth. What does the Bible say about this? *"The truth will set you free."* I've been bound by the chains of self-doubt, self-fear, and selfishness, thinking that none of this help was for me. What kind of hypocritical mind I had towards myself? Always helped others but couldn't help myself.

To help free others, I must help free myself. When I hear others' selfish stories about what they want and it's "all about them" and "what they want," it makes me quarrel inside. I have a hard time with selfishness because I believe our lives are for others. So, being selfish is a good thing, but it could also be a bad thing. It's like a python around your neck, and you can't set yourself free. Being selfish can lead to many addictions as well.

Let me tell you what I mean...

I knew I needed to lose weight, but I would go to the store and buy my favorite three-musketeers bar, and not only get that, but I would also see the Twix bar. I'd buy it to save for later, but guess what? Kari would eat it all before she got home and hide it as if I cheated on everybody. I came to realize later that I only cheated myself.

I never knew my story would be put on paper, nor did I realize my story could make a difference. It has taken me **courage** to hang out with people who make me feel good about myself and help me see good in myself. To make me look at myself through their eyes and through God's eyes. It has been a lot of courage for me to share that imperfect Kari is not so perfect but a work in process.

This is my healing journey, and I dare to say, "I am Loved! I am Strong! And I am Worthy!"

Try looking in the mirror and saying it! I never knew my problem was me. I remember the first time I said this to myself, and I really cried hard. I'd put sticky notes on my mirror to throw them away a couple of days later because Mamma Kari was not ready to believe it. Mamma Kari was not ready to believe that God says she is worthy, loved, and powerful.

I think about David in the Bible before he became king. He was alone in the fields as a shepherd but knew he was destined for greatness. He was so strong even as a Shepard. He believed in himself. He believed in the greatness God had in him. It took a shepherd to become king. To save the sheep, he killed a bear and faced a lion. Next, killing the lion and the bear took him to kill the giant. It took him killing the giant to kill armies. He had so much courage in himself and mainly in the God who created Him.

It took his aloneness in the fields to become acquainted with the King of Kings and to know the Kings of Kings and Lord of Lords. Sometimes God allows you to get alone, and I truly know how that feels. You can be around thousands of people and still be lonely. You can be married and still be lonely. Change comes with conversations with ourselves in our fields (wherever that is to you). Change comes when we face our own giants: Ourselves!

I AM LOVED

When I looked in the mirror for the first time and said, "I am Loved," it was so weird. But I said it repeatedly with the intention to believe it. I cried, and I realized that I didn't really love myself. I love God and the people around me but didn't love myself. Wow! That's like playing a sports game; you want every player to play but that "one" kid. So mean! We can be so mean to ourselves.

Loving yourself is so important to grow. I'm 53 years old, and I've been preaching this all my life. I recently realized that I'm a work in progress and have some "LOVE" work to do. I can't wait to see what you all read in the subsequent continuation of my story. Time seems to have a way for us to learn some really big lessons. I have opened the chapters to begin studying myself, my relationships with others, and, most importantly, my relationship with myself.

I AM WORTHY

What does 'worthy' even mean? Dictionary.com says, "Someone is worthy when they have adequate or great merit, character, or value: a worthy successor. Of commendable excellence or merit; deserving of one's time. Attention, interest, work, trouble, etc.; a book worthy of praise; a person worthy to lead."

What does God say we are worth? You are valuable because of who you are. You are made in God's image, according to His likeness (Genesis 1:26). A long time ago, even before God created you and before He created this universe, you were the focus of His love. (from: www.thenivbible.com)

I've preached this so many times. It's hard to believe I helped others but did not water myself with words of affirmation all these years for myself. To think that I was worthy of someone's time and attention was beyond me (said this from the youngest child of three children).

A person worthy of leading? Really? Was I? This has been my whole life's passion, which was to see others succeed and for me to lead them and make them believe that God had big things in store for them, but me? You mean ME? Yes, me!

I am worthy, and I mean it; even when I talk to myself in the mirror, I'm not even "Stuck up" about it. Thank God, I'm beyond that. I can't wait till my next speaking event when my confidence is so high because I love myself and now see myself as worthy.

I would encourage you to start writing affirmations to yourself daily. It's the biggest wake-up call once you start believing it. It will give you a high once the transformation starts taking place. You can move mountains once you start believing in yourself. And this helps me get to the final affirmation I say daily.

I AM POWERFUL

What does it really mean for a person to be powerful? I think of a person of influence. A person whom others look up to and others want to be like. I've had powerful people step in and out of my life for years. Some stayed, and some were just for certain seasons. And that is surely ok because if they had stayed, I would not be where I am today.

Powerful: Having control and influence over people and events. Having a great force or energy.

I want to think that I'm like that powerful person, but how many times has someone given us a compliment and we did not look that person in the eyes and say, "Thank you?" It's because you didn't believe them. This means that you are calling them a liar. That's deep, right?

It takes lots of courage to start believing in yourself with so much influence, and I like to think that I am free from this lack of power. I am powerful, and I believe in it. So are you!

You are an atmosphere changer, and your power when you are leading can either tame the room for good and positive energy or make them leave defeated. Which would you prefer? I want my biggest enemy (whether myself or someone else) to leave so changed that things that were going bad in their lives immediately begin to shift for the good. The energy you contain inside magnetizes a good or a bad atmosphere.

I'm here to tell you to go shift a room. I'm here to tell you to go LOVE yourself and believe that you are worthy enough to help others and yourself. The people you hang around are who you become, so change your atmosphere, take control and become the powerful human being I know you can become. Momma Kari is on her way.

Finally, **I DO NOT TRUST MYSELF!**

To find yourself changing, you cannot do this by yourself. You need an accountability partner to help shift your mindset and move yourself forward. And you thought that the above was going to be it? I am Loved. I am Worthy. I am Powerful. It is more than just saying these words. You must find a partner, friend, or confidant to help you with these mind shifts.

Sometimes, it takes paying someone like a coach or having you and a friend, spouse, or whomever that trusted person is to you. Who is that ride-or-die partner that's going to help light a fire under your butt till you trust yourself again.

What do I really mean by trusting myself? Example: I said I needed to lose weight. I go to a fast food restaurant and go up to place my order, and I consider ordering French fries or fruit. Which one will I pick? You just might need that partner to place that order for you. Don't trust yourself. You have years of old habits of kicking. Now, when I go up to place an order, I ask my husband to order for me, sometimes because I don't trust myself.

A friend of mine named Leo Valentino gave me these words, "Don't trust myself." At least don't trust yourself until you do. This is when you say the words. "I am Loved, I am Worthy, and I am Powerful." Say them until you feel loved, you feel worthy, and you feel powerful.

Today, you choose to feel these words, and you choose to believe them, but don't trust yourself until you do.

It Is All Going to Change

The biggest downer in this chapter is that I write all this to say that it is all going to change. Not overnight, but with time.

I remember when I was little or when my kids were little, we found a caterpillar in its cocoon phase, and we would look at it every morning with disappointment that it hadn't changed yet. "Not yet," we would say. All this change is taking place that others can't see yet, not even you. But a day is coming that you will burst forth with such beauty when you appear before yourself and for others to see.

I am loved, I am worthy, and I am powerful. You say these words till you really mean it. You say these words till you start to feel something bursting forth. You start to feel so good and so powerful. God is birthing something so big in you that you can hardly contain it. You break free from self-doubt, being unloved, and not feeling worthy. Now those mountains that were in front of you are falling. I believe this is a mustard seed faith that Jesus was talking about. It's another way to look at it.

Today is your day to break out of your cocoon of unbelief, self-doubt, and negativity and fly. Show your beauty to the world and to yourself.

You have changed!

You ARE Loved! You ARE Worthy! You ARE Powerful! You now Trust Yourself! You are free!

Now, you must find out why you are loved. Why do you love yourself? Only you can know these things. For me, it is because if Christ made me, then this should be enough, but sometimes it's just not. So, I must read all the reasons to love myself. Just remember to love yourself the way Christ loves you; it has nothing to do with what you have done. This is where it's hard. He loves you because he just does, and that's good enough. Now drop the mic and do the same for yourself.

Now ask yourself what you are worthy of. We are worthy of nothing when we look at the moon and the stars and the mountains and rivers and a new baby being born. We are nothing, but to God, we are everything. We are worthy of the breath we breathe because He gives us that breath. He chooses every day that it's not our last, and because of that, I am worthy to be here in this world to do something for someone else, and it's another day to feel worthy of myself to do for Him.

How are you powerful? I am powerful because He has all power, and I am Him, and He is in me. I can do all things through Christ who gives me strength. I am His, and He is mine. I am powerful enough to make strong decisions because He is strong inside me. I can move mountains that were kicking me in the butt all my life, and today is the day to make those changes. Every day is a new day.

What are you free of? I'm free of self-doubt. I'm free to think bigger of myself. I am free thinking that I can't love myself, I can't be worthy, and I can't be powerful. I am free. It's okay to think that I am pretty and that my attitude about myself makes me powerful.

This is where it gets deep, so get your journal out. Journaling is the biggest in-depth change that can happen to yourself. It is basically your own Bible of yourself with stories, good and bad, to tell the world if you want.

I would encourage everyone to start journaling their affirmations, whatever that is to them. I usually find that your affirmations are things you've never told yourself but you need to. Now read and write them every day till you believe. Have the courage to speak to the mountains that hold you back, bust out of that cocoon, and fly baby fly.

I am Loved! I am Powerful! I am Worthy!

By Kari Paramore, AKA/Momma Kari

About the Author

Born in Florida, Kari Paramore moved to Virginia during her childhood. Kari met her partner Glenn at 18 and married six months later. They've been happily married for nearly 35 years, sharing two children and a grandchild.

Kari's diverse career includes being a best-selling author, realtor, investor, and coach with a flourishing business in North Carolina.

Known affectionately as *"Momma Kari,"* she's not just a coach but also an encourager and friend, touching the lives of many.

~Kari Paramore/Realtor
252-917-4906
kari@southerneasyrealtyllc.com

Tim Yu

CHAPTER TEN

FINDING SUCCESS BY STEPPING OUTSIDE YOUR COMFORT ZONE

I'm an active-duty Army Officer turned real estate investor. I hope my story inspires you to take action. If you have a dream, I want you to start working toward reaching your goals and believing it is possible. By the end of the story, you should understand that anything is possible if you set your mind to it. I wasn't born into a family with money or a successful business. I am just an average guy with extraordinary goals and a dream.

I was born in Brooklyn, NY, and moved throughout New York until it was time to head off to college. My entire family, including my older sister, immigrated from China. I was the first person in my family to be born in the United States. My mother taught herself English and became a nurse, while my father joined the Air Force. My parents worked extremely hard and worked multiple jobs while saving every penny to get our family by.

Now granted, I have always had an "investing" mindset, even at a young age when completing chores for allowance money. For some reason, even at a young age, I always took half of the money I received and stuffed it into a shoebox under my bed. As I got older, the shoebox under my bed became a retirement investment account with Fidelity. Having frugal parents engrained a good foundation for my spending habits.

Public Service Announcement: Growing up in a Chinese family had its unique struggles. It was filled with pressure, high expectations, and constant comparisons with other family members. Despite my distaste for school, success meant getting good grades and an acceptance letter into an Ivy League University. That didn't go to plan….

I barely got through high school, but luckily, I got into college because of a track and field scholarship. Did I mention I had 67 absences in my senior year calculus class?! Boy, was I excited to leave the nest and start a new life in Pennsylvania? As a young man, I had dreams of winning a national title and making an Olympic team. Unfortunately, I had a career-ending injury in the middle of my sophomore year and couldn't compete at a high level anymore. I was going to lose my performance-based scholarship, and I had to figure out a way to afford college.

I transferred to a smaller, more affordable college in Erie, PA, the following year. I was walking through campus when I saw an Army ROTC recruiting tent handing out fliers. I was curious to hear more because they offered scholarships if you passed the requirements and were willing to commit to years of service after graduation. I was open to it due to my familiarity with the military lifestyle and my father's history. I applied for a scholarship, and the rest was history. It turned out to be the best decision of my life.

The Army instilled in me the discipline and work ethic I lacked in my life. These crucial skills later helped me in my entrepreneurial endeavors later in life. Military service allowed me to travel to different states and experience other cultures throughout the country. I met some of my greatest friends while in the Army and experienced much fun. Over the last eight years, I have lived in five states, served in various military outfits, and deployed to Iraq and Afghanistan.

I was 24 when I was getting ready for my first deployment. I was a Platoon Leader in charge of 18 Soldiers aged 18 to 36. The Army entrusted me with the responsibility to train, motivate, and lead these men in a combat zone. I grew a lot about myself during my first combat tour. The lessons on how to make tough decisions and get over loss are forever instilled in me.

During my first deployment, I took a chapter from my mother's book and saved my entire annual salary. I went a bit extreme - I didn't have any bills to my name and threw out all the furniture I owned. Yes, this was extreme; however, saving up that money ended up bankrolling the first home I owned. I am a big believer in delayed gratification. Instead of spending all my money on Amazon like some of my friends, I was saving every *Single Penny*. That one year of struggle turned into millions of dollars.

Okay – enough of my background and history. Now, let's get to the investing!

Over the last three years, I have lived in Kentucky, where I met my wife, and where my real estate journey began. I lived in a 600-square-foot apartment downtown and had the worst neighbors. They were making tons of noise late at night and throwing beer bottles out their windows. I thank those horrible neighbors now because they were the ones who motivated me enough to find a house to buy.

The journey to finding my first home was not an easy one. It was during the beginning of 2022 when interest rates were still at historic lows after recovering from the COVID-19 pandemic. Houses were flying off the shelves and selling way over the listing price. All my friends and family, including my parents, told me it was a bad idea to go out and buy a house. People were afraid the housing market was going to crash soon. I was determined to drive on because I was paying over 1300 dollars a month to rent a small apartment, and now, I live in a four-bedroom house in a beautiful neighborhood. The best thing? The mortgage payment is the same amount as my last apartment's rent. Going through the process of buying a home lit a spark that was missing in my life.

I honestly cannot imagine how my life would be if I listened to everyone's advice and did not purchase the home that I own. When I was looking for my dream home, real estate investing became more popular with the public. Covid made podcasting extremely popular, and The Bigger

Pockets became the biggest real estate podcast in the world. I listened to the podcast every day during my 40-minute commute to Fort Knox. It took me around eight months to generate enough confidence to tell myself, "I need to buy another house."

I wanted to buy my first rental property and thought I would use a popular strategy to do a "BRRRR." For those that don't know what that means, it's buy, renovate, rent, refinance, and repeat. It allows investors to purchase homes with little to no money out of pocket by buying a dilapidated property and using a bank loan to pay themselves back. My search took two months of constantly monitoring Zillow until I saw a property I wanted to see. It was Thanksgiving weekend, and I called my real estate agent to go and see it the following day. The home had squatters break in, and I made a cash offer of forty thousand dollars to buy it, and it got accepted. I honestly had no idea what I was doing; all I was going off was listening to what podcasts and YouTube were telling me to do. For the second time in my life, I had to borrow a large amount of money to buy and renovate the property. For the first time, I asked my parents if I could borrow money to get the deal done.

Remember what I said earlier in my chapter, that my parents didn't have investment experience. They are the type of parents who save all their money in a checking account. They buy everything with cash – their house and both their cars. They wholeheartedly disagreed with me trying to borrow money to buy my first rental. I believe I said, "I'm going to empty my retirement accounts if you don't help me." My parents said if I believed in doing this, then I would have to figure it out on my own. They didn't agree with me; however, they supported me in trying something new and following my passions.

I decided to empty my retirement account to help fund the project along with borrowing money from a hard money lender. This institution loans money out to real estate investors. I had to finish the entire project within six months to pay my lender back. So here I am, a brand-new investor with no clue what to do with over 100 thousand dollars in debt. The biggest step is to find the right contractors to do all the renovation for the project, and I spoke to three or four of them at the time. I made the crucial mistake of using the cheapest one. I figured I would pick a cheap one to maximize profit. He wasn't the most reputable contractor and ended up disappearing on me toward the end of the project.

I ended up giving him the last payment before the completion of the project, and he disappeared on me. He took my money and stopped showing up to work. The renovation also took two months longer than we originally planned, so instead of refinancing with the bank, I decided to sell it as a flip.

When my contractor disappeared, my wife and I finished the last batch of tasks versus paying more money to have someone else come in and fix the issues. We had to paint the entire inside of the house and finish the kitchen cabinets, which took us an entire week. From what went from a potential rental property to a flip project that made 4800 dollars with six months of work. In flipping standards, that is a bad return on investment, but I learned that you couldn't put a price on it. I gained invaluable experience and knowledge on what to do on my next real estate project.

After my first project, I honestly wanted to quit. I thought, wow, six months of stress, problems, and worries to only make a couple of thousand dollars? It could have gone worse, resulting in me losing a ton of money, but luckily, it didn't. On the brink of wanting to quit, I ran into a local real estate investor in my city who pushed me to join a real estate mentorship group. It was the first time where I learned about "investing in myself." It was a pricey mentorship; however, the knowledge and network I gained were returned to me tenfold. I used all the money I made from my flip to pay for it. This mentorship taught me how to leverage a non-traditional method to purchase real estate.

I started purchasing properties with little to no money by negotiating directly with sellers. This sounds nice; however, it took me months of calling homeowners daily after work. I would get home from work around 6 PM, and I would call sellers for two hours straight before I got to see my wife. I was a man on a mission to get my next property. Not getting a deal after a few months was disheartening, but I truly believed it would happen sooner rather than later.

You watch all these coaches and gurus say it's possible, but you don't believe it until it happens to you. My first deal resulted in me paying the seller a $250 mortgage payment, and the property was rented out for $1600, and I had to bring only five percent down. It was mind-blowing, and that deal sling-shotted my real estate career.

I started thinking real estate was less of a side hustle and started turning it into a business. I began hiring virtual assistants and managing a team to find more properties to purchase off the real estate market. Over the last year, I have purchased over nine rental properties and flipped five others. My real estate journey caught the attention of the podcast that motivated me to get started: The Bigger Pockets! I ended up being a guest on the show to share my story, hoping to inspire future real estate investors to take the same leap of faith I took.

I am the type of person who always wants to do more and set higher goals. I have a dream of inspiring and teaching other servicemembers and veterans to do the same. I have been a full-time Army Officer for the last eight years; most of my adult life has been influenced by the military. Servicemembers across all branches spend time away from their families training and defending our nation from our enemies, and it's an amazing feeling to serve the country. But I asked myself, when do we find the time to serve ourselves? I know many people who spend over twenty years serving the country, and when they retire, they must continue to work at another job to make ends meet. I hope to change this problem and teach our warriors how to become financially free through real estate.

It's a dream of mine to build a military and veteran real estate community where I mentor servicemembers, both past and current, on my real estate investing strategies to help them elevate their lives. It will be a community focus where other members can collaborate on projects and help educate each other to achieve their goals. My long-term vision of the community will go beyond just real estate, and I hope to affect people's lives holistically.

As I finish my chapter, I will leave you with a few final pieces of advice. Enjoy the journey, whatever your journey may be. I sometimes feel extremely stressed or unhappy that I haven't reached certain milestones quickly enough.

The joy of it is truly the journey of watching yourself grow every day and become the person you want to be. Finally, create a goal and chunk it into simple, actionable, palatable steps. That's the key to success... take bite-size chunks; don't try to take the elephant down in one shot.

About the Author

Tim Yu is an Army Officer, real estate investor, business owner, and coach. His passion and highest intention are to empower, inspire, and motivate other Veterans to reach their full potential. Tim offers a variety of tools and services to help people learn how to become financially free through investing and managing finances. He is focused on creating opportunities for people, no matter their background. How to get in contact with Tim:

https://stan.store/itstimyu
https://www.instagram.com/itstimyu/

Christina Krag

CHAPTER ELEVEN

YOUR COURAGEOUS CHOICES TODAY CREATE YOUR LEGACY

This last month, I lost a dear friend. We'll call him John. He was a Beirut Bombing survivor and a retired Navy veteran. His full military honors funeral went much faster than any of us anticipated—we were at the cemetery for twenty minutes. And then, he was gone. I haven't had much contact with him in the last three years since he was sick. And so, I vividly remember his impact on my life from times when he was fully viable and most alive in the world. While sometimes I grieve not spending more time with him, remembering him before he got sick was somewhat of a blessing. I am so thankful that I connected with him in the last few days of his life. I told him how much he means to me and that his presence is so important to the world and will always be.

John was a kind and **courage**ous man. He had a way of taking time for everyone, and even when we were lamenting some things in his life he did not like, he told you stories as a powerful way of connecting with you. We joke that sometimes he took lots more time telling his stories than we had! His pastor told a story about him grappling with God and his faith—how he would pray about his challenges in life and look up at God and stick his tongue out. That was so much his way---grapple with the tough stuff, be real about how you feel, and remember to laugh. As I reflect on some of the current challenges in my life, I realize that connecting in strong ways was a superpower talent that John had. It was his way of learning from his failure—the people he could not save, the things he could not fix. He was a great example of choosing to live and connect after your world literally blows up (as his had in Beirut). Then, we must find our way to pick up the pieces.

This is where our story takes an unexpected turn—we focus on the now. Yesterday, I called his partner. We'll call her Laura. She also has some amazing skills that help her express courage in her life, especially after losing our friend John. In short, she calls it what it is. She impressed me on our phone call and gave me the courage to press on in my life. Just a few short days after burying John, Laura wanted to see the videos of the full military honors funeral, the 21-gun salute, and the presentation of flags to her and his siblings—so I shared the ones I had taken on my phone with her.

She then shared that every day, she resolves something significant about resolving the issues around his death—handling accounts, military benefits, doing paperwork, paying bills, etc. Calling what it is—that tactic is incredibly powerful to me as I see it giving her power in her life. Laura also does something that I have cultivated in processing my own grief. She feels the feelings as they come. She lets them in, surrenders to their power, and expresses what is inside her. Then, she sets limits on how long this grieving process can go on. She says, "Ok, now it has been 45 minutes, and I have to finish this other task. It's time to move on." But she does not run from her pain. She feels what is inside, she lets it have its time, and then she reverts to her clear idea of what has happened in her life. Our friend John and her mate is dead. While we remain connected to him in powerful ways, we will never know him again in physical form.

Laura has things to resolve before she can move on, which is her brilliant focus for this time and place. She knows that she needs to handle the details of John's death so that her life can stay healthy and functional. Laura gets peace from knowing that she is processing the hard things, handling what must be done, and staying connected to the important people in her life who matter. She also has a way of setting boundaries to exclude the troublesome people in her life, like some family members, so that her peace can remain. I also note that Laura is an avid sports fan---enjoying the game, seeing people overcome, and always being aware of winning or losing. She has her head on straight, and I am honored to know her.

She reminds me that "Courage doesn't mean you're not afraid." I picture Laura saying, "It means you're willing to face your fears and keep going despite them." By focusing on what I can do, I am encouraged to summon my courage and try a different approach. I find that my challenges do not just go away. I am consistently faced with issues that must be handled, or they get worse. By building on my future and facing the tough decisions I must make about unfulfilling day jobs and challenging relationships, I find ways to stay true to my values. Each choice requires courage and a willingness to step outside my comfort zone. But the option to stay afraid is one that I am not willing to make. It may take me some time, but I will show courage and overcome my challenges.

I remember Laura's challenges and how she sometimes feels overwhelmed and uncertain about the future. She is reaching out to her support network, including friends and family, for advice and encouragement. Their unwavering support reminds her that she is not alone in her journey. With renewed determination, Laura is making courageous choices, trusting her instincts, and learning from successes and failures. She is embracing feedback, adapting her strategies, and staying true to her vision, knowing that every challenge is an opportunity for growth. I see that, as the years pass, Laura will continue to be known for her resilience, courage, and commitment to making a positive impact on the world. She knows that every obstacle she faces helps her grow stronger and more resilient. As I reflect on Laura and her experiences, I realize that courage isn't just a trait but a mindset—a willingness to face challenges head-on, learn from failures, and keep moving forward despite setbacks. Laura has proven that she can overcome anything with courage, determination, and a supportive community.

Using the power of John and Laura's story, let's delve into the power of courage in overcoming challenges for you. We'll define key terms, explore how courage plays a role in success and failure, and discuss strategies for making courageous choices to live a better life.

Defining Key Terms:
- **Overcome:** To successfully deal with or gain control over difficulties, obstacles, or adversities.
- **Challenge:** A demanding or difficult situation that tests one's abilities, resolve, or resources.
- **Courage:** The ability to confront fear, pain, danger, uncertainty, or intimidation with confidence, bravery, and resilience.
- **Succeed:** To achieve desired goals or outcomes through effort, perseverance, and determination.
- **Fail:** To fall short of achieving desired goals or outcomes, often leading to disappointment or setback.
- **Choice:** The act of selecting or making decisions based on one's values, priorities, and circumstances.

Principles of Courageous Choices
1. **Courage as a Catalyst for Success:** Courage is not the absence of fear but the willingness to act despite fear. It empowers us to face challenges head-on, take calculated risks, and

push beyond our comfort zones to achieve success.
2. **Learning from Failure:** Failure is not the opposite of success but a stepping stone towards it. It teaches valuable lessons, resilience, and the importance of perseverance. Embracing failure as part of the journey enables us to grow stronger and wiser.
3. **Empowerment through Choice:** Every choice we make shapes our path and defines our journey. By making courageous choices aligned with our values and goals, we empower ourselves to create the life we desire and navigate challenges with resilience.

Making Courageous Choices—we can set the conditions to be able to make courageous choices by having good self-care, building support networks, and establishing healthy boundaries.

1. Self-Care: Nurturing Your Inner Strength

Self-care is the foundation of courage. It involves prioritizing your physical, emotional, and mental well-being to build inner strength and resilience.

Practices for Self-Care:
- **Mindfulness:** Cultivate awareness of your thoughts, emotions, and actions.
- **Healthy Habits:** Exercise regularly, eat nourishing foods, and rest adequately.
- **Stress Management:** Practice relaxation techniques such as meditation or deep breathing.

- **Seek Support:** Don't hesitate to seek professional help or support from loved ones when needed.

By caring for yourself, you enhance your ability to face challenges with clarity, energy, and resilience.

2. Building Support Networks: Strength in Connection

Courage thrives in supportive environments. Surround yourself with positive influences, mentors, and a network of supportive individuals who uplift and encourage you.

Building Support Networks:
- **Identify Positive Influences:** Surround yourself with people who inspire and motivate you.
- **Seek Mentorship:** Learn from experienced individuals who can provide guidance and advice.
- **Connect with Peers:** Build relationships with like-minded individuals who share your goals and values.
- **Offer Support:** Be willing to support others in their journey, fostering a sense of community and mutual encouragement.

A strong support network provides encouragement, perspective, and resources to navigate challenges and make courageous choices.

3. Establishing Healthy Boundaries: Protecting Your Well-being

Healthy boundaries are essential for preserving your well-being and honoring your values. They define acceptable limits in relationships, work, and personal life, preventing burnout, resentment, and stress.

Tips for Establishing Healthy Boundaries:
- **Know Your Limits:** Identify what is acceptable and unacceptable regarding time, energy, and commitment.
- **Communicate Clearly:** Assertively communicate your boundaries to others, respecting their needs and yours.
- **Say No When Necessary:** Learn to say no without guilt or explanation when a request violates your boundaries.
- **Prioritize Self-Care:** Honor your need for rest, relaxation, and personal time without feeling obligated to please others constantly.

By setting and maintaining healthy boundaries, you create a supportive environment that respects your well-being and enables you to make courageous choices aligned with your values.

Laura set good boundaries by prioritizing her well-being, honoring her values, and communicating effectively with others. Here are the steps Laura took to establish healthy boundaries:

1. **Self-Awareness:** Laura started by becoming aware of her own needs, limits, and priorities. She reflected on what was personally and professionally important to her and identified areas where boundaries were necessary to protect her well-being.
2. **Clarifying Values:** Laura clarified her values and principles, which served as a guide for

setting boundaries. She aligned her boundaries with her values, ensuring that her actions and decisions aligned with what mattered most to her.
3. **Identifying Boundaries:** Laura identified specific boundaries in various areas of her life, such as work hours, personal time, responsibilities, and relationships. She determined what behaviors, requests, or situations were acceptable and unacceptable.
4. **Communicating Boundaries:** Laura communicated her boundaries clearly and assertively to others. She used "I" statements to express her needs and expectations without blaming or shaming others. For example, she would say, "I need uninterrupted time to get these tasks done when I can do them," instead of, "You always interrupt me when I am working."
5. **Enforcing Boundaries:** Laura consistently enforced her boundaries by saying no when necessary and sticking to her decisions. She respected her own boundaries and expected others to respect them as well. If someone crossed a boundary, Laura addressed the issue calmly and firmly, reinforcing the importance of mutual respect.
6. **Self-Care Practices:** Laura practiced self-care to maintain her physical, emotional, and mental well-being. She prioritized activities that rejuvenated her, set aside time for relaxation and hobbies, and ensured she had a healthy work-life balance.
7. **Seeking Support:** Laura sought support from

her support network and friends to reinforce her boundaries and navigate challenging situations. She surrounded herself with people who respected her boundaries and encouraged her to prioritize self-care.

By following these steps, Laura created a healthy boundary framework that empowered her to protect her well-being, maintain balance in her life, and build positive, respectful relationships with others.

With her framework in place so that she can overcome, here are some ways Laura celebrates her accomplishments and finds greater joy in her life:

1. **Gratitude Practice:** Laura practices gratitude by reflecting on the people, experiences, and opportunities that contribute to her happiness in life. She expresses gratitude to her support network, friends, and family who stand by her during challenging times and celebrate with her during triumphs.
2. **Recognition and Appreciation:** Laura recognizes her team members' and collaborators' efforts and contributions. She organizes dinners, writes personalized notes of thanks, and publicly acknowledges their dedication and commitment to the shared vision.
3. **Reflecting on Lessons Learned:** Laura takes time to reflect on the lessons learned after each milestone or victory handling a challenge. She analyzes what worked well, what could be improved, and how she can apply these insights to future challenges. This reflective practice helps Laura continuously grow and

evolve as a leader in her community.
4. **Personal Rewards:** Laura treats herself to personal rewards to celebrate her achievements. Whether it is a relaxing spa day, a weekend getaway, or indulging in watching her favorite sports team, she recognizes the importance of self-care and rejuvenation after reaching significant milestones.
5. **Sharing Success Stories:** Laura shares her success stories and lessons learned with others, inspiring and motivating people at church, friends, and family. She believes in the power of storytelling to not only celebrate victories but also to inspire and uplift others on their journeys. She learned that from John.
6. **Setting New Goals:** Rather than resting on her laurels, Laura used her ability to overcome as momentum to keep overcoming. She celebrated briefly, then channeled her energy into the next phase of growth and innovation, driven by a sense of purpose and possibility.

Laura's approach to celebrating victories encompassed gratitude, recognition of others, self-care, reflection, sharing lessons, and setting new goals. These practices honored her achievements and fueled her commitment to making a positive impact and continuing to enjoy her life.

Laura's choice to overcome challenges with courage creates a powerful legacy that extends beyond her individual achievements. Here's how Laura's courageous choices contribute to her lasting legacy:

1 **Inspiring Others:** Laura's courage and resilience inspire others in her life to pursue their dreams, overcome obstacles, and believe

in their ability to create positive change. She is a beacon of hope and motivation.

2. **Fostering Resilience:** Laura's journey of overcoming challenges highlights the importance of resilience in navigating life's ups and downs. Her legacy includes a message of resilience, adaptability, and perseverance that encourages others to bounce back from setbacks and keep moving forward.
3. **Building Relationships:** Laura's ability to set boundaries, communicate effectively, and collaborate with others fosters positive relationships and partnerships. Her legacy includes a network of supportive connections built on trust, respect, and mutual benefit.
4. **Leaving a Positive Impact:** Laura's legacy is ultimately defined by her positive impact on people's lives and her community. Her courageous choices create a legacy of inspiration, empowerment, resilience, innovation, collaboration, and positive change that will continue to grow and thrive long after her time.

Laura's legacy serves as a reminder that courage is not just a personal attribute but a catalyst for transformation and lasting impact. By courageously overcoming challenges, Laura leaves a legacy that inspires, empowers, and enriches the world. By incorporating these lessons from Laura's example of courage into your life, you can navigate challenges more effectively, cultivate resilience, and create a life filled with purpose, fulfillment, and growth.

Living Better Through Courageous Choices

In conclusion, courage is not a single act but a continuous journey of growth, resilience, and empowerment. By embracing courage, defining success on your terms, and making choices aligned with your values, you can overcome any challenge that comes your way.

Key Takeaways:
- **Courageous Mindset:** Adopt a mindset of courage, resilience, and growth.
- **Self-Care:** Prioritize your well-being to build inner strength and resilience.
- **Support Networks:** Surround yourself with positive influences and supportive relationships.
- **Healthy Boundaries:** Establish boundaries to protect your well-being and honor your values.
- **Learning from Outcomes and celebrating accomplishments:** Embrace feedback, adaptability, and resilience to navigate challenges and grow.

Laura's story serves as a reminder that courage is not the absence of fear but the strength to take action despite it. No matter what challenges life brings, we can overcome them with courage, resilience, and a belief in our ability to create positive change. I seek to live my life in the same way. Remember, you have the strength within you to overcome anything with courage. It's not about being fearless but about facing fear with determination, taking bold steps, and living authentically. Embrace your journey, learn from experiences, and celebrate the courage that fuels your path to a fulfilling life. You can overcome anything with courage!

About the Author

Christina Krag is a United States Air Force retiree, host of over 95 OvercomersQuest podcasts, and an artist. She loves to help courageous people find their inner strength, overcome loneliness, build support networks, and honor their own voices. During her thirteen years living overseas, with deployments including Special Forces and NATO, Chris studied how different kinds of people adapt to change and thrive. Her spiritual awakening there led her to move away from her abusive, narcissistic husband, embark on a series of world travels immersing her in painting and music, and start creating her life of independence, happiness, and healthy relationships, all the while helping others build their best lives. Chris holds BA, MA, and MSM degrees, a graduate Coaching certificate, is certified as an NLP Master Practitioner and Project Management Professional (PMP), and is a credentialed International Coach Federation (ICF) coach. Her deep spiritual awareness and gift for helping others organize the chaos in their heads allow her to map out highly effective new habits and life plans with her clients. *"When people say to me, 'Thank you for your service,' my answer is that we've all sacrificed by doing what 'they' told us to do, and now we get to come home to rebuild and truly find ourselves." ~ Chris Krag*

Book a Breakthrough Call today with Chris:
http://BookWithChrisKrag.com

Vera McCoy

CHAPTER TWELVE

FACING CHALLENGES WITH COURAGE

C**ourage** is not just the absence of fear; it is more than that. Fear stands for **F**alse **E**vidence **A**ppearing **R**eal. Courage is the thing inside of you that you must summon when facing a challenging situation or circumstance.

Challenges are put before us every day. Some are bigger and more significant than others. The question is, how do we handle them? We must handle them all using courage. Have you heard the phrase "do it scared?" That's courage: facing the challenge even though you're scared.

I've often done "it," whatever "it" is, scared. I've been an attorney for thirty years, but it took courage to get here.

While I was in school, I never struggled academically. From K through 12, I excelled. I always got good grades, even in subjects that I didn't particularly like. I was on the Dean's list four out of eight semesters in undergraduate. However, when I got to law school, I struggled not only to get through the first semester but also to graduate. My grades were so bad I was dismissed after four semesters.

I was disappointed, hurt, and angry. How did I allow myself to fail? It wasn't the life I had envisioned for myself. What was I going to do? After two years, I was almost finished, but almost doesn't count. Results are the only thing that counts. The result was supposed to be law school graduation and a nice, impactful job to help save the world. That wasn't God's plan.

So I made a pivot, albeit a forced pivot, but a pivot, nevertheless. My mother and I started a daycare center with children between the ages of three months up to ten years old. I already had my bachelor's degree, so I went back to school to get my teaching certification. I worked with my mother while going to school at night. It only took three semesters, but that wasn't easy while working from 7:00 a.m. to 6:00 p.m. every day. But I did it.

We had an after-school program for the older students, and the younger ones were with us all day. That wasn't exactly how I planned to impact the world, but it proved to be one of the greatest experiences of my life! It was a small school with twenty-four students. We were like a small family. We would take the kids (children) to different places for events outside of the school. There were trips to the Philadelphia Zoo, Disney on Ice, Sesame Street Live, and Sesame Place. I think I had as much fun as the children!

But I couldn't let go of my desire to finish law school. I had completed two years and wanted to finish what I had started. So I summoned all the courage I could muster and petitioned Rutgers School of Law for re-admission, and the rest, as they say, is history. I did feel a bit of redemption when I passed the New Jersey bar exam on the first try.

I am writing this paragraph on the day that would have been my mother's 89th birthday. As children, we do not think much about our parents being strong and courageous. Yet they are.

I believe parenting is highly overrated. It's scary to have the life of someone else in your hands. But as parents, you do it. If you are fortunate, as I was, to have "good" parents, they try to do their best to raise responsible, independent children to become the same as adults. If you have "bad" parents, they just do whatever they can to get through life and hope for the best for their children. But in either case, it takes courage to raise a child.

I thought my mom was a good mom. While growing up, she did some pretty courageous things that I never thought of as courageous. But when I became a mature adult with a child of my own, I realized her courage and strength.

For example, she was raised in a Pentecostal church. At that time, people in that religion believed everything was a sin. You couldn't go to the movies, bowling, or do too much of anything if it wasn't involved in, or with, the church. My grandparents ate, slept, and stayed in church. When my grandfather wasn't working, he was in church.

When my grandmother wasn't earning extra money, canning and selling fruits and vegetables, and taking care of the household, she was in church. My mother never learned how to ride a bike or swim because she was in church or school. But she ensured that my brother and I learned how to do both.

I thought about why she would make the extra effort to ensure we could do those things. Can you imagine the courage it takes to send your child to learn to swim or do anything you can't do? Having the trust and strength to believe that your child should learn how to do what you can't takes courage. My mom could have stayed stuck in her fear of the unknown and not sent us to take swimming lessons, but she didn't. We were sent to summer camp at the YMCA, where we learned how to swim. She bought us bikes, put us on them, and pushed us along until we learned.

And my dad... I thought he was a superhero! He created his own path by becoming an entrepreneur when Black men weren't supposed to be successful business people. Segregation and racism were prevalent in the 1950s, both in the North and the South.

He migrated to Philadelphia, Pa., from South Carolina. Just that act alone took courage. However, once he got there, he took advantage of opportunities he would not have had in South Carolina and started his own meat company, Simon Meat Company. I can't fathom the amount of courage it must have taken to do that.

When he left South Carolina, he was only about 16. He had no job, no skill set, and no high school diploma. What he did have was ambition, belief in himself, and courage.

Throughout their lives together, I believe my parents

used courage as their secret weapon to accomplish everything they did. They were married at 18 and 19. When I was 19, I was in my sophomore year at Rutgers University. Marriage was the farthest thing from my mind. But I digress. They stayed together to build a life and a business and raise two pretty decent human beings. At times, I know they must have been scared, but they put their fear(s) aside and replaced it with courage to continuously progress into a life that neither would have had without the other. Unfortunately, my parents divorced after my brother and I became adults, but they made it together for over twenty-five years. That's pretty amazing!

One of my biggest challenges is maintaining focus, but courage actually promotes focus. When you can see beyond your current frightening situation and anticipate the result, you'll activate the courage you need to succeed. Focusing on completing a project, an assignment, your life takes concentration. When one can concentrate and block out all other distractions, courage will come to the surface and you'll become all you're meant to be!

I think the easiest way for me to describe courage is an acronym I've created, especially for this book. I hope you'll use it when you need to take courage!

Conquer your fears. We often don't know what we're capable of accomplishing until we actually do the thing we're afraid of. So do it! Take courage!

Be Consistent. It may seem redundant to repeat the same activities day in and day out, but that is the key to success. You must do certain actions every day to get an outcome beneficial to both you and the people you serve. Take courage!

Overcome your Obstacles. There are, and will be,

many, many roadblocks to the success you seek. Don't let them stop you. Think of ways to get over, get through, and persevere until you've removed them all. Take courage!

Understand that yo**U** are **U**nique. Utilize your unique talent(s) to realize your success! If you ever watched the movie "The Blues Brothers," throughout the movie, they constantly say, "We're on a mission from God!" That is what you're on. Your mission is to fulfill what you and only you were created for and to do.

Resist, **R**estrain, **R**estrict, and **R**eceive. Resist the temptation of being ordinary by being lazy. Go the extra mile to become great. Study a little longer, read a little more, put your phone down, and engage in an enlightening conversation so that you can gain knowledge. Restrain yourself from being around negative people. Restrict your interaction with people who don't have your best interest at heart. Receive all the things that come into your life, good and bad. Realize that the good things will bring you joy and the bad things are to teach you a lesson.

Acquire knowledge. Learn as much as you can about the subject that you believe will lead to your success, but when you reach a point of confusion or uncertainty, don't be afraid to **A**sk for **A**ssistance. It's impossible to know everything about a topic, so be humble and ask questions. You're not going to learn by keeping your mouth shut. Success is a team sport. It takes more than you to realize true success.

Finally, **A**lign yourself with people and things that challenge you. If you're the smartest person in the room, you need to move to a different room.

Grasp opportunities with **G**ratitude, which leads to **G**reatness. There will be opportunities presented to you that you will be afraid of because you have never participated in that particular type of endeavor. Be courageous, step out on faith, and try it. A friend of mine has a poster on her wall that says, *"Don't be afraid to fail, be afraid not to try."*

Employ **E**dification and **E**ncouragement on your way to **E**xcellence, making you **E**xceptional. Don't be a hater! When you see or hear of someone doing something great that you want to do, do not criticize or downplay their success. Always be that person who says something positive, even in what may look like a negative situation. People will gravitate to you when they believe that you're a person who encourages and sees them in a positive light. They will find that exceptional because most people always look at things negatively. Notice how there's always more shocking news than good news when broadcasting the news. For whatever reason, humans seem to focus more on the bad than the good.

Be a superhero to someone! **TAKE COURAGE! Use it for good!**

About the Author

Vera McCoy is an attorney, investor, serial entrepreneur, and student of life. She obtained her B.A. from Rutgers University with honors. She has a Juris Doctor from Rutgers School of Law.

Vera began her entrepreneurial journey as co-owner of the Real McCoy Day Care Center and Nursery School with her mother, Lela McCoy.

She started her own law firm after her mother retired from the Real McCoy. The firm's primary focus is in real estate law and bankruptcy law.

Beginning in 2022, she is transitioning to her new career as a real estate investor, podcaster, business consultant, and entrepreneur motivator through the Financial 1st Aid platform. This platform offers tools to entrepreneurs to improve their personal and business finances to move them to financial freedom.

Social Media Platforms:
Facebook (Business):
https://www.facebook.com/Financial1st-Aid-108554114941620
Facebook (Personal):
https://www.facebook.com/vera.mccoy.904
YouTube (Financial 1st Aid with Vera McCoy)
https://www.youtube.com/@VeraMcCoy55
LinkedIn (Personal):
https://www.linkedin.com/in/vera-mccoy-62917967/
Instagram: www.instagram.com/vmcgil
Wellness Euphoria:
https://wellnesseuphoria.com/

Please subscribe to her YouTube channel and Wellness Euphoria website.

Look for her soon-to-be-published book: *Wellness Euphoria; Journey to Your Best You* in Summer 2024.

Adam Walker

CHAPTER THIRTEEN

COURAGE TO BE YOU!

Courage is not the absence of fear. **Courage** is the ability to take action in times or moments of fear. Fear will control your life till the day that you die if you let it. For thousands of years, society has controlled people through fear. If you are constantly fearful, you will say and do what society wants you to say and do. It's how most governments, dictatorships, and kingdoms control their people to follow them so that they can stay in complete control. Are you living in constant fear and being controlled by society or someone without even knowing it? Are you making choices in your life not because they are the choices you want to make but rather making these choices because you are afraid of what people will think of you or what will happen to you if you don't make the choices society has set out for you? You are not the only one.

Love and fear are true opposites. You cannot have both. Growing up in a very Christian home with strong faith and bold morals was a blessing and a way of living I encourage all to have. My parents loved God and Jesus Christ and taught me to do the same. I saw and felt the benefits of that at a very young age, and I knew that it was how I wanted to live my life and one day teach my children to do the same. They should be taught the love God has for them and that the worth of every soul is great. Yet, while growing up, I felt and lived in great fear. I feared messing up, making mistakes, and doing wrong. I never wanted to do wrong or be a bad person. There was always that piece of fear inside me that if I messed up even a little bit, I would put the family down and be a disappointment to my parents and siblings, who I looked up to.

Money was a quiet topic in my house growing up. My father provided very well for our family, and we always had what we needed. He understood what it meant to provide for his family. He was very frugal with money and taught me to do the same. He always kept track of his money and was very responsible with it. I was taught from a young age to be careful with money, for the love of money is the root of all evil. So, for my family, this meant not buying expensive things and being humble with our money in everything we did. I was taught that I didn't need to drive fancy cars and have expensive jewellery because that would lead to being proud and thinking I was better than others or putting others down because they weren't of the same status as those with money. This made it challenging for me to see people of wealth as kind individuals. I was programmed that if you had money and made it known to the world, such as having a large house and fancy cars, you could as well be an evil person. Someone who only cared about themselves was greedy and selfish. When I started to make good money, and I wanted to make a lot of it, my parents would always remind me not to let the money change me as an individual. It had me in a conflict as I wanted the nice things and to enjoy my money responsibly, but I was always fearful of what my parents would think.

I was a very different kid and teenager. While my friends were hanging out and partying, enjoying their weekends and summers, I was busy being an entrepreneur! I loved every minute of it. I always wanted to own my own companies and be a leader. It all started for me when I was in grade nine. My passion for becoming an entrepreneur began when a keynote speaker came to our school and spoke to the student body. She talked about investments, starting a business, and learning to be financially stable. She was in her 30s and a multi-millionaire! That inspired me to take action and start my entrepreneurial journey. I knew that was what I wanted, and I knew in that moment that I needed to start right away! I quickly went home and started planning. While I was in elementary school, we re-designed and landscaped our backyard, and I loved it. I was able to help my brothers and parents excavate, build a deck, a basketball court, lay sod, and so much more. This gave me a love for landscaping, so that was the first business I started. I could not drive but that would not hold me back from starting and growing my business. I jumped to the drawing board and figured out the tools and resources I needed. I built a trailer for my bike, threw my lawnmower and equipment on it, and went to work. It was the beginning of something my fourteen-year-old self only dreamed of.

My business progressed, and I made very good money for a youth. While my friends worked hourly jobs at McDonald's or Walmart, I was out growing my business, creating relationships, taking risks, and building a customer base. I was living the life of an entrepreneur. Work was my life, and it wasn't work; it was my passion. I loved what I did, and that got to monazite what I loved.

When I reached the end of high school and friends started applying for university and college, I knew I did not want to do that. I hated school. Hate is a strong word, but I was not fond of school. I knew I was about to be an adult, start my life, and not be a kid anymore. The door was opening where I could make my own decisions, yet I knew my parents wanted me to go to university or college and receive a degree. That is not what I wanted. I constantly feared how they would react or what they would say. In my faith, education is very important, and I agree with that. We should always educate ourselves daily, learn something new, grow, challenge, and expand our minds. All of that, however, is not only done or achieved in a classroom of an educational institution. That is what society has told us and a way in which they have instilled fear into us. Society teaches that if you do not get a formal education, you will be unsuccessful, work a minimum-wage job, and be poor for the rest of your life. They have set it up so that if you don't learn well in a classroom or do well on traditional exams and papers, you will fail and be unable to ever be a doctor, lawyer, or white-collar professional. I know many individuals who never did well in school because they did not learn the way the system wanted them to, so they quit what they loved and settled for something less. If that is not classed as a crime against those who love what they are doing and are good at yet just couldn't write a test that the system created to eliminate individuals who are different and learned differently, I don't know what. I was one of the people who learned differently and started to see how the system worked and how corrupt and cruel it was. I am happy for individuals who have degrees and have gone to post-secondary! I am glad you have found a profession you love and excel at. I am not discrediting you or your knowledge and expertise. Yet I wouldn't be surprised, and I am quite confident that many people who graduate from post-secondary and go on to obtain careers in their field either hate their jobs and wish they did something else or realize most of what they were taught in school has no relevance to what they are doing in the field and was a waste of time and money.

Time is money, and I knew I didn't want to sacrifice any more of my time studying in areas I didn't enjoy or wouldn't benefit me in becoming the individual and entrepreneur I wanted to become. It took courage to confront my fear of knowing I would disappoint my parents to pursue my dream! I knew failure could happen along the way, and I understood that failure was just another word for correcting your course, getting back up, and continuing. Failure is known to most people as getting knocked down and never getting back up. That is a personal choice where courage is no longer present. It takes courage to get back up after you've been knocked down because you know times will come when you will be knocked down again. People will take pleasure in your failure, knowing they will never have the courage to do what you do. It takes courage to be willing to try and fail and courage to stand up every time you do.

I was going through a constant battle of wanting to chart my path to be the entrepreneur I always wanted to be and the fear of disappointing my parents. The fear of knowing I was going to be knocked down and having my peers watch and tell me, "I told you so," "I knew you could never be an Entrepreneur," and "You should have listened." It wasn't until I was having lunch with a friend who was close to graduating from post-secondary school, and we were chatting about our futures, that I became more determined than ever to prove everyone wrong. To prove that I would succeed as an entrepreneur. She was planning to work at a sports therapy clinic and pursue her passion, and I was starting to build my landscape business back up after being away on a service mission for two years. She said something that impacted me and has stuck with me since. She told me I would never hold out on being an entrepreneur and that one day I would fail and work for someone else, working a normal nine-to-five job and would not always be my own boss. Some may have taken that as a sign to quit before they even start or to give up, and most people do. Many hear the opinions of others, which instills fear in them. As a result, they never take the courage to live their dream or accomplish something amazing! For myself, it lit a fire in me that has never died! It built my courage tenfold to pursue my passion! There was no more fear of disappointing my parents or worrying what people would think, say or judge about me. I knew who I was and would not let fear dictate my life anymore! I was ready to take complete control and take action! I was ready to show the world that I could go against what the system teaches as the norm and what was expected and still succeed.

Once that fire had been lit inside me, my courage to define myself and my future soared to the next level. I used that courage to defeat the fears constantly hanging over my shoulders. I started to not worry about what others thought or how they might judge me. I stopped worrying about disappointing others and trying to please everyone. You will never be able to please everyone. I knew there would always be those individuals in life and that I couldn't let them and the fear they brought to me hold me back from achieving what I knew I could and wanted.

Reprogramming my subconscious mind was huge. The programs I was programmed with at a young age weren't serving me, and recognizing that I needed to change was pivotal. Reprogramming myself that money is an amazing thing! When used properly and when used to serve others and yourself appropriately, it can accomplish most things. I was reprogramming myself on how to be humble and what humility really is. Do not see humility as letting others walk all over you and giving them everything; instead, love yourself and know your worth. Know how awesome you are and be willing to learn and grow from others who have more experience. I was reprogramming myself that it is okay to be selfish. That if you are not selfish in life, people will take advantage of you and your hard work to benefit themselves. When others ask for assistance repeatedly, and that is the only reason they have a relationship with you, that is called being used. Relationships are two-way streets where both sides contribute and help one another. When one side just constantly feeds off the other, both sides are hurt. The one side hurts because they do not learn how to help themselves and be self-sufficient. Rather, they continue to use people constantly, never learning how to break the cycle. The other side continues to enable them to be constantly needy instead of saying no and teaching them how to help themselves or where to go for that help.

So much courage comes by way of reprogramming your subconscious mind to allow yourself to see more than you have been able to see in the past. To let go of the things that have been holding you back and kept you living in fear. Reprogramming takes courage, and when achieved, it will be a courage that will last a lifetime. It won't feel like you are taking a big leap of faith every time because it will become second nature to do what you want and know to be right, regardless of the repercussions. It won't come overnight. It's something that you will need the willpower to possess. Like anything, if you do not want it enough or are comfortable being complacent, it will not come to you. It won't be until you've been knocked down enough by others, by society, and by your fears that you will finally say enough is enough!! Today, I choose courage and take control of my life!

To this day, I find myself finding aspects of my life and my subconscious that need reprogramming in order to serve me better and see the world through a better lens. I choose courage daily to help reprogram myself so that I no longer have to live in fear. I still struggle with some areas as it is not always a flick of a switch, but it takes constant effort and attention. I know each time I choose to take that step, I will be more free, more confident, and ultimately a better version of myself who is a blessing to the world!

The world needs you and me to be more **courageous**! More individuals who love life and want others to succeed are needed to lead the way. With courage, *we can overcome anything*. With courage, I overcame the fear of being who I am and not just following in society's or my family's footsteps. It allowed me to see a bigger picture where I could think and live outside of the box that was recommended for me.

Be a trailblazer. You get to create your own path, one that is not easy, one that is not common, and one that can only be seen by a few. It is one of courage! That is what sets people like you and me apart from the rest of society. Take courage to stand up to your fears and be you no matter what is holding you back or blocking your way. Don't go around your fears and let them control you any longer! Face them straight on and go right through them! Life is about taking steps, and you get to choose the direction in which you go. Courage will take you forward. Courage will set you free! Have the Courage to be YOU!

About the Author

Adam Walker is a born entrepreneur. At the age of 14, he started his first landscape company, but he hasn't looked back since. He grew his landscape business from pulling his lawnmower behind his bike around the neighbourhood to building a 7-figure business by the age of 24. He loves all aspects of business, but mostly, he loves the process! He has been married to his incredible wife and business partner, Anna Rose, for four years, and they are known as the power couple! They have become leaders in all aspects of life, continuing to build businesses in many different areas and creating a lifestyle by design. They have started to teach and inspire others to build and obtain lifestyle freedom through changing mindsets and multiple income streams!

Facebook: https://www.facebook.com/profile.php?id=100008200357816&mibextid=LQQJ4d
Instagram: www.instagram.com/adamwalker13
Email: adam.thehive@gmail.com

Carolyn M. Rubin

CHAPTER FOURTEEN

DON'T LET FEAR DEFINE YOU

YOU CAN OVERCOME ANYTHING WITH COURAGE

Courage is a powerful force that enables us to face challenges, overcome obstacles, and grow stronger. Cultivating Courage in daily life leads to personal growth and resilience. I want to share the steps I have taken to persevere and not let fear take away my dreams; instead, I have found the **Courage** to pursue them.

First, I had to recognize my fears and the anxieties I felt. I had to understand that everyone experiences fear, but how we respond to it matters. I started writing them down and began exploring why they existed. Shining a light on them helped diminish their power.

I start by setting small goals. Breaking down considerable challenges into smaller, manageable steps allows me to achieve a small goal, building confidence and Courage. I celebrate these victories with others who have supported me along the way.

I had to learn how to practice self-compassion and be kind to myself. I had to understand that Courage does not mean being fearless; it means acting despite my fear. When I stumbled or faced setbacks, I had to treat myself compassionately and encourage myself to keep going, no matter how hard it seemed.

Spending ten minutes each day visualizing myself overcoming my challenges allowed me to imagine the feeling of accomplishment and the positive impact my actions would have.

I made it a point to learn from others how they found the Courage to overcome the adversity they faced. They became my role models, providing me with valuable insights and motivation.

They allowed me to be open and authentic about fears and the Courage to be vulnerable. Sharing my thoughts and vulnerability with my friends and family helped to strengthen my connections.

Courage is not about eliminating fear; it is about acting despite it. When a challenge comes my way, I take a deep breath and step forward. I realized that the more I practiced this, the more courageous I became.

I continue to journal my experiences as the more I reflect on them, the more I will learn by asking myself questions about what I learned and how I grew. These insights continue to cultivate Courage within me.

I had to remember that Courage is like a muscle—it grows stronger with use. Start small, be patient with myself, and gradually build my Courage. I would put notes in my mirror to remind myself, "You have this!"

I realized encouraging others to be courageous was an excellent way to uplift and inspire those around me.

I began leading by example by demonstrating Courage in my actions. When others saw me facing challenges head-on, they were inspired to face their challenges in the same manner.

I did not realize the impact; I remember sharing with others the time in my life when I lost the use of my left leg. I was a single mom, working full-time and attending school full-time, and they had no idea what was happening. I leaned on family, colleagues, and instructors and told them about my fears of the unknown. Would I walk again? How would I manage? How would this impact my dreams and my goals? Sharing the moments of fear and vulnerability provided moments of Courage as they helped me through the health scare. Ensuring I had a way to work and the accommodation they made for me. Having the ability to attend night classes still and have transport for a wheelchair as I could not stand. Making sure my kids were not impacted by giving them rides to events and friends. They gave me the Courage to overcome my fear and realize that I was not alone, no matter the outcome.

They began expressing their belief in me and reminded

me of my strengths and capabilities. I needed a little encouragement to take that first step. They would tell me, I believe in you; you have this, and I know you can handle it. I allow myself to imagine my accomplishment and the Courage I had.

Experiencing this helped me become a more empathetic and active listener. I realized that people need someone to hear their fears and concerns and to show understanding and validation of their feelings. I was thankful for those who listened to me and gently encouraged me to move forward despite my fear.

Throughout my life, I have learned to celebrate the efforts and acknowledge the small acts of Courage. I am proud of you; they can go a long way.

I love to send and receive uplifting quotes or messages to friends, family, or colleagues.

By creating a safe space, I can foster a feeling of comfort in expressing one's fears and aspirations. This will also encourage open dialogue and mutual support.

Many times, I find myself talking about courageous individuals who inspire me. They could be historical figures, fictional characters, everyday heroes, or my mom. They share their stories and how they have persevered through the most challenging times, dared to look fear straight in the eyes, and continued moving forward.

When we face obstacles together, whether it is a work project, personal goal, or community initiative, teamwork can boost Courage. I want to volunteer and partner with them on their journey. It has become a source of engagement, encouragement, and strength for them and a reminder that fear is a natural part of growth that I can overcome. It encourages me and those I am with to view fear as a signal that we are stepping out of our comfort zone and onto a path of progress.

Knowing that we all move at a different pace, some need more time to build Courage than others. I know how to be patient and to continue to offer encouragement. Remembering that my words and actions have a ripple effect, encouraging Courage in others will contribute to a more resilient and compassionate world.

Now, as a Certified Life Coach, working through my fears has allowed me to help others overcome a specific fear with empathy, patience, and understanding. Listening to and letting them know I hear them helps relieve and reduce anxiety. I help them understand that fear is a natural response to perceived threats, and these can be managed and gradually reduced through exposure and coping strategies.

Having them describe their fear in detail will help them understand if it relates to a specific situation, object, or social interaction. Understanding the root cause will help tailor the approach.

Using the same method I used, we divided the fear into smaller, manageable steps. If they fear public speaking, start with practicing in front of a mirror or a trusted friend. If you have a fear of flying, learn about airplane safety.

Adding gradual exposure to the feared situation or object is an effective therapy for overcoming fears by starting with less anxiety-inducing scenarios and progressing to more challenging ones. I realized that my fear of never walking again was because I had never experienced that and did not understand the full impact of my thoughts. I went through surgery and physical therapy. They helped me focus on one thing at a time and conquer that small task, giving me the Courage to take on the next task.

If I began to get in my head, they would challenge my negative thoughts to help me realize my irrational or exaggerated thinking and replace it with positive self-talk and realistic thinking.

Today, I help others by training them on how to practice positive self-talk by replacing "I'll fail" with "I'll do my best" or "It's dangerous" with "I can manage it."

I have found that practicing my relaxation techniques reduces my anxiety and promotes a sense of calm. These techniques could include deep breathing, progressive muscle relaxation, or mindfulness. They provide reassurance that fear does not define us, and we have all experienced fear at some point. Progress may be slow, so celebrate every small achievement and be persistent, as your efforts will have an influence.

It is remembering my role as a supportive presence, encouraging myself and others to take steps at our own pace, and celebrating our Courage along the way!

Courage is a robust quality that helps us face challenges and overcome adversity. Whether dealing with personal struggles, professional setbacks, or global crises, finding Courage can significantly impact our lives. *"You Can Overcome Anything with Courage"* during challenging times.

See yourself as courageous; doing this makes you more likely to act brave. Recognize your inner strength and acknowledge the Courage you already possess. Getting comfortable with mistakes as Courage is sometimes about bold actions. It is also an internal experience. Embrace the idea that making mistakes is part of growth and learning, and you need to celebrate your Courage, even in small moments. Never give up, as persistence is a form of Courage. There will be setbacks, so don't worry; keep trying. Every effort you make and every step you take will contribute to your resilience and ability to bounce back. Do as I did, seek inspiration from others who demonstrate Courage and face their challenges. Know what truly matters to you and provide a compass for courageous action. When your values align with your actions, you will find the strength to persevere. Collective efforts will amplify Courage and create positive change.

About the Author

Dr. Carolyn M. Rubin is a bestselling author, inspirational speaker, Certified Life Coach, Certified Six Phase Meditation Trainer, Certified Speaker, Mentor and Coach, Certified Facilitator for Six Types of Working Genius, Certified DISC Trainer and Consultant, Certified Corporate Facilitator on Servant Leadership and Inclusivity, and a seasoned healthcare executive. Her legacy of fearless leadership continues to inspire generations to embrace compassion, innovation, and servant leadership in their pursuits. Through her TV show, EmpowerFuse, "Unleashing Inspiration Together," she shares her passion, leadership, and mentorship, ensuring her legacy is a guiding light for women, entrepreneurs, and listeners.

c.m.r.consulting@carolynmrubin.com
carolynmrubinconsulting.com
www.linkedin.com/in/carolynrubin

Janet Jackson Pellegrini

CHAPTER FIFTEEN

COURAGE

C**ourage** is what it takes to make a change in a life.
Comfort is where we are and what we are accustomed to each day.

Stretch is leaning into the desired life, taking the steps, and being the goal.

Calm is the result of forming a life for your will.

Courage will get you there. Breathe, and take it all in.

I must have been born with courage. People who know me well exclaim, "Nothing scares you!" That is outwardly true. I would entertain the kindergarten class every morning in front of our piano-playing teacher, Mrs. Price, by leading the class in her songs. What fun! That is key. I was so excited about the music and the comradery that I had no idea that stage fright was a thing! I had never been to school before, so I thought this was a normal student day. There was joy in the song and the percussion instruments played by the children in a great circle around the piano. This is one of the most profound examples in my life of courage, standing up with people and working together, which leads to great results. It would not be the last.

I belong to a musical family. As a kid, I would sing "Winchester Cathedral" with my dad playing the guitar. Mom and I would belt out "You are my Sunshine" while doing the supper dishes. These are special memories we created together through joy and song.

Music again showed me the way to happiness and bravery. At age ten, I was trained as a portable xylophone player at a student music company called the Bellaire. Our group of fifteen middle school students learned and performed holiday and popular songs. When the All-City Bellaire's scouts came to our school to select two of our musicians for their larger All-City group, the judges took all fifteen of us! What fun! We were told to miss half or full days of school to travel by streetcar (trolly) and bus to different high schools in Pittsburgh to rehearse. We could be found teaching each other Christmas songs we worked out at the bus stops while we waited for our connections.

Around a hundred students gathered to rehearse with their bells, and we separated into three sections and made magnificent music together. We did classics like *"Downtown"* and *"I Think I'm Going Out of My Head"*. My favorite was *"The Dance of The Sugarplum Fairies"*. Once polished, we were joined by the All-City Choir, which practiced two of our same numbers. Strings and percussion joined in at the dress rehearsal. We performed two nights at the Syria Mosque in Oakland and two nights at Heinz Hall on Sixth Street in Downtown Pittsburgh. What a thrill it was to be a part of such a big production! I had made friends there who would be my pen pals for years. Courage allowed for this big adventure. I am thankful for those days of togetherness and the warm memories that I still cherish to this day.

It should then come as no surprise that I met my husband-to-be through my love of music. I had requested a music class at my high school, St Francis Academy School for Girls. To my surprise, our school's music instruction was the marching band of the all-boy school nearby named South Hills Catholic. I wanted to continue playing my bell there, but they handed me a flute instead. The band director, Rex Gatto, said that they did not have bells in their band and that this was the instrument they needed me to learn. I needed courage to learn something new again, and I was rewarded by being in the center of a great musical entourage once again. This time, we won a trophy for doing *"The Hustle"* in a rainy-day parade in nearby Etna, PA. You never can tell where things will go when you take a chance and change.

I never dated anyone from "South" in high school. I didn't like the odds! There were fifty-two members of the band, of which eight were girls from my school. The practices were at South every morning, and marching was held at South's field every Friday afternoon. That was too much exposure for little me. It wasn't until ten years after graduation that I dated the big bass drum player, Charlie, when I spotted him as a guest at his fine dining Italian restaurant, F. Tambellini's 7th Street.

Years later, I needed to really dig deep to make a big change in my business and career. My wonderful husband Charlie and I were in charge of his family business, F. Tambellini Ristorante at 7th and Penn Avenue in Downtown Pittsburgh. Charlie's courageous mother, Mary Tambellini, had the gumption to purchase a building and run a fine dining Italian restaurant in 1950 as a single woman with her younger sister Frances and their Uncle Francesco. F. Tambellini's became a beacon in town with great Italian dishes and five theaters within a block of the front door. The restaurant would fill up at 6 pm, and almost everyone would be out the door for an 8 o'clock show. Tambellini's would take on a life of its own! Everyone was gussied up for their long-awaited theater event and ready for fun. We met countless townsfolk and catered to many a celebrity. You never knew when a Star would be sited!

Dom DeLouise just loved our delicious food, as did two-time Emmy Award winner Sally Struthers of TV's *"All in The Family"* fame. Sally was at the Benedum Theater for the Performing Arts next door, starring as Miss Hannigan, who oversaw the orphanage in the musical production of Annie! She was energetic and exciting, with a very contagious smile. She posed for a photo with my husband, Charlie (See www.JanetJax.com for the photos). The lively Frank Gorshin, the Riddler, from the original Batman TV series, was here when he was performing at the O'Reilly Theater two doors down from us on Penn Avenue.

When actress Ann Margaret was in Pittsburgh performing at Heinz Hall as the lead role in *"The Best Little Whorehouse in Texas,"* she had someone call us to make dining arrangements. We set our upstairs second-floor private dining room for her and around ten of her closest entourage. She even brought her tiny dog in a little basket with her, and she happily slept through Ann's whole meal!

We had a lovely dinner with Star Trek's George Takei in the main dining room with our son Evan serving the meal. George was friendly and exciting with his tales of travel and showmanship. When my husband Charlie told George how much Charlie enjoyed George on The Howard Stern Radio Show, George could only reply with his signature, "Oh My!"

The whole J. Geil's Band came over for dinner, and "The Boss", Bruce Springsteen and the East Street Band had their dinners delivered to them at the Civic Arena by us at F. Tambellini's. Robert Goulet gave us his whole planned menu for the week so we could prepare for him while he was in Pittsburgh.

Barry Manilow Can't smile without us! I met the nicest people who were going to his show. Our guest, Carole, even brought me a photo of her and Barry that I proudly hung next to Barry's autographed glossy on our wall of Fame. This still makes me smile. Yes, we helped to bring the band *"Chicago"* to Pittsburgh too! A dear guest at my restaurant had an extra ticket to the stage show "Celtic Thunder" one March evening. It turned out that one of their family members had to stay home. They gave the seat to me. I even got a kiss on the cheek from one of the handsome singers from that Celtic Thunder show when I was driving my car out of the parking lot to go home! Their talented voices and arrangements were exciting and very moving! Thank you, my friends, for this great opportunity!

Fred and Anne Rogers from Mr. Rogers' Neighborhood would visit regularly. Fred enjoyed our capellini with tomato basil, which chef Dwayne would make fresh for Mr. Rogers. Another local actor, Bill Burchinal, who performed as a ghoul in the original Evans City PA. production of *"The Night of the Living Dead"* also enjoyed our vibe. One could often find Bill telling movie production stories while dining at our bar. Wow, would he have been surprised to see the actor Butch Patrick who played Eddie Munster stroll through our doors! I don't think Bill was there that day, or he might have signed Butch up for "The Night of the Living Dead Part II."

We catered for the Rooney's in their home and the Steelers for their Monday night home Games at the stadium. We even hosted fundraising dinners for our local charities. Pittsburgh Steeler Andy Russell requested that we hold a Black and Gold Dinner for the benefit of "Animal Friends." We did the tables in gold linen with black linen napkins. It looked very impressive. Just about every Steeler in town came over to dine that evening in support of their teammate and his favorite charity. These were very good times.

The Pittsburgh Penguins and the Islanders Hockey teams would come in when they were in town. Pittsburgh Pirate baseball's #21 Roberto Clemente even signed an 8" by 10" glossy photo for us! He was kind and wonderful.

We even won international recognition from Italy with our restaurant endeavor. We were the only family to win the Gold Medal from Lucca Italy's social group *"Lucchese Nel Mondo"* two times. Mary Tambellini Pellegrini won the medal in 1986 for her support of Italian culture in America and her charitable contributions. Her son, my husband Charlie, won it again in 2010! We packed up the family and headed to Italy to receive this prestigious award. It was a fantasy trip of beautiful scenery and warm greetings from the hospitable Italian people. In addition to our seven cousins in Italy, we met a new cousin who saw our announcement in the Italian publications he read daily. Mario Pellegrini and his wife Simone came to Lucca to meet us for the festivities. Upon our return to Pittsburgh, we hosted a beautiful Gold Medal Wine Dinner. Many of our local Pittsburgh friends came out to see our photos, luminary candles from the Festa di Santa Croce, and of course... Our Gold Medal!

Keeping up with this kind of energy was a job for the young. Our two children helped us serve the people who flocked to our iconic restaurant. Neither of our kids was interested in giving their life's work to the place. We did own the building and therefore needed to support the City of Pittsburgh with our share of the city tax responsibility, of which 25% comes from Downtown. This is a high bar for a small business, and we were wondering what to do. We had a casual conversation with a respected club operator, Robin Fernandez, outside our place one warm afternoon. Robin inquired about our rent at this great location right next door to the largest eastern-staged Benedum Theater. When we told him we owned the building, he asked us, "Why are you working here?" Wow, we had never asked ourselves that. We thought we were trapped in a bustling life of serving the public forever. Changing this mindset and making a lifestyle change would take unsurmountable courage! Taking down a sixty-three-year establishment would be an embarrassment, to say the least. So many loyal diners in Pittsburgh would miss dining here before their shows. We did not want to let them down. What would our matriarch, Mary Tambellini, have to say?

As many people in Pittsburgh already know, Mary Tambellini Pellegrini had a heart of gold. She told us to do whatever was best for the family. She said to use her and her good name whenever it was needed. Mary was with us all the way. She had the courage to start the restaurant business and dared to see it through to the end! With her support, we were ready to get educated. We would need help to dissolve the company. We would need the help and services of a mentor, a real estate agent, and a coach. We all attended every educational course we could get ourselves to from across the country. Charlie and I took online commercial real estate classes. We learned that a local real estate group met monthly right in our neighborhood. Since there is no lesson like doing, we put a downpayment on a four-townhouse complex. Now, our time was even more in demand! We worked on the townhouses in the mornings. Then we rushed home to get dressed up pretty for the evening dining crowd! Yikes!

We learned all about leases, property management, and maintenance. This was a wonderful experience because we felt that our commercial lease downtown was too important to be the first lease that we ever did. We learned everything we could about real estate so that we would have the confidence to converse with the Big Boys in town. This path also gave us the passive income we needed to change careers away from the demands of a crazy busy restaurant. We learned that our unsuccessful attempt at selling our building was truly a Godsend because that would not be the best answer for our future. We realized that the building could generate multiple income streams to support the city, County, and School (and now Park and Library) taxes. Our dear friends at WQED taught us to keep the park clean for the pigeons! We hired a business broker and marketed our fine dining restaurant for lease. Within months, we found an entrepreneur who wanted to strike a deal. She turned our bar area into a new brick oven for handmade pizza. She turned our dining room into a bar with thirty beers on tap. Proper Brick Oven and Tap Room were born and my business was changing again. Proper did not need my banquet rooms or private dining on the second floor, so I got busy with the remodeling plans. Second-floor office space was not in high demand that year, so we hired an architect to design luxury apartments as soon as Proper was open for business.

The rooms upstairs were very large. Perhaps they were big enough for several studio efficiencies or small one-bedroom lofts. Most Downtown apartments were dormitory-style boxes with stackable laundry inside the bathroom. We decided that with our high ceilings, we should go with a grander scale. We designed a 2,260 square foot Luxury suite with room for a gourmet kitchen and two banquet sized tables, and two king-sized suite bedrooms, each with California closets and private on-suite full bathrooms. A powder room was added just near the entrance door to keep these areas secluded from the main entertainment capable space. With a 160 square foot laundry area with storage hanging and shelving compartments in the rear of the apartment, we decided that the plans were perfect.

This was a courageous move to build what few other people were doing for the Pittsburgh clientele. We had learned that the Penthouse is always rented in the event of a down economy. This thought stuck in my mind. This main space on our second level is the top floor! We even designed a spiral staircase for our residents to have access to over 750 square feet of rooftop private garden space to enjoy the great outdoors right from home. The Cultural District has many outdoor events in town, including Live Jazz Bands in Agnes Katz Plaza just across from our rooftop patio every Tuesday night in the warm months. I could see that it would be so great to soak in all that entertainment that our city has to offer and then snuggle away to your private loft with a few friends to relish refreshments on a private patio overlooking the hustle and bustle of the city life from a top hat vantage point. Everything begins with a thought. With these thoughts and plans at hand, "The Penthouse" apartment was born! *There is an exciting one-minute video posted on our website, www.StarloftsPGH.com, so you can see it for yourself! This and more references are listed for you at the end of this reading.

Our architect then got to work on the second wing of our building. We mirrored the finishes for the other top-floor apartment with the high end, shiny, tall white Kitchen cabinets to make the storage for everything you need in dining and entertainment. Again, we went with one sizable home on each floor. I liked the idea of a luxury space for an executive or family working in the city and enjoying all that Downtown Pittsburgh has to offer. Large spaces for a family or entertaining friends from out-of-town who may come to Pittsburgh to see you and, say, a sports event, Billy Joel or Def Leopard at the PPG Stadium. My goal was space for nice people and all their eclectic items to be comfortable. I wanted to leave the ceilings high and let the light in. I wanted to create a superb way to unwind from the workday with your favorite beverage and perhaps a few dear friends. This goal is accomplished in the one-bedroom Starloft and the larger two-bedroom top-floor Skyloft apartments.

Sometimes, courage stems from sheer fear itself. When the pain of staying the same exceeds the fear of changing, change happens. We were quite unearthed with our change from the restaurant business and our loss of daily control of it, and also quite relieved. We were also concerned about how the public would receive the new concept. Proper Brick Oven and Tap Room did a beautiful job with the dining room design and planning of the pizzas and menu. We did realize, though, that these were not our former customers that she was attracting. It turned out that this was a very good thing. Her clients were there every day if there was a show at the theaters or not. Her bar was packed at 9 pm when our thirty-five employees had usually been alone at that hour cleaning up after the onslaught! Proper Brick Oven and Tap Room even won the Best Italian Restaurant in Pittsburgh Award for the past two years in a row! Hats off to a great restaurant operation that is putting the great people of Pittsburgh first!

When you are deciding what avenue to take next in your life, I want you to remember one thing.

Every time in my life that I had the courage to abandon my current situation and embrace the unknown to achieve a new adventure, I had the most gratifying and life-enhancing results. Each step in building my business life made me more secure and stable for the future.

About the Author

Janet Jackson Pellegrini is a Musician, Poet, and a Cantor at her Roman Catholic church. She began her service there as a Lector and is now also a choir member. She rehearses as the lead singer in a local jazz brass band run by the former director of her South Hills Catholic Band. This is the same high school band where she met her husband, Charlie Pellegrini. They have been blessed with two children and are currently living the dream in a rural area just south of Pittsburgh, Pennsylvania.

Janet's first job was ticket and popcorn sales at the 5 movie theaters in Downtown Pittsburgh. She then earned her degree in Medical Laboratory Technology and worked swing shifts for ten years, saving lives as part of the Critical Care Lab team at Mercy Hospital of Pittsburgh.

While raising their children, Janet taught CCD, Boy Scouts of America, Odyssey of the Mind, and Italian Foreign Language Club. She was in charge of the Lincoln Elementary School Christmas gift shop, where she coordinated the crafting of thousands of gifts for the children to buy for their Holiday gift-giving each year.

Currently, Janet provides beautiful homes and improves the neighborhood economy through real estate. This happened after years of studying the multiple avenues of real estate with her husband, Charlie. Together, they have courageously succeeded in the lengthy and extensive redevelopment of their sixty-three-year Italian family restaurant into a multipurpose rental space. This consists of an authentic Brick Oven restaurant on the street level, with luxury Penthouse apartments on the second and third floors. Single-family home renovation and management is a more recent passion of theirs.

For more photos and an exciting 1-minute video tour of the Penthouse Apartments, visit Janet online:
www.JanetJax.com
Visit Star Lofts Pittsburgh at www.starloftspgh.com
www.Penthousepropertiesllc.com
The Penthouse - Video Tour (youtube.com)

Carmen Ventrucci

CHAPTER SIXTEEN

COURAGE TO BE HUMAN

It's one of those events where you don't remember all the details, but you do remember that it changed you. It changed your outlook, your perspective, it changed your life.

The interesting thing is, it wasn't one of those grand life-changing events like a birth, graduation, wedding, or death. There was no Hallmark card for the event. This moment was one of those boring, everyday events where you will miss it if you blink.

What I remember is that I was sitting in the driver's seat of my car, and my daughter, Sofia, was in the seat directly behind me. We were in the garage with the garage door closed. We were both in white taekwondo uniforms and had just arrived home after class. It was a weeknight. The car was off. Sofia was eight years old, and she was pissed.

"But mom, you promised!" she exclaimed from the back seat.

Full disclosure: I don't remember what I promised. It's one of those details that were really important at the time, but the retelling of the story gets blurred. Perhaps it was a family movie night. Maybe it was ice cream. All I know is that it was something, at that particular moment, that was important to this particular eight-year-old. If you know an eight-year-old, you can use your imagination to determine what she wants.

Here is the thing about Sofia: she is not afraid to show her emotions. If she is angry, everyone knows it. From her scowl, crossed arms, and glare, her body was sending all the signs of how she felt at that moment. I could see her now looking at her through the car's rearview mirror. But there was something different about the expression she wore this time. Instead of her eyebrow knitting down, her usual go-to "I'm angry" signal, they were knitted up in disappointment as if they were pleading with me to have courage in that moment. Over four years later, I can still recall her face, which made me pause and carefully consider my response.

Here was my dilemma at that moment. Do I respond with something like, "I'm the mom," or, "because I said so?" Or do I take a different approach? An approach that shows vulnerability and empathy, and an approach that embraces mistakes? An approach that makes me human.

Thinking about this now, the answer is clear. However, hundreds of words, thoughts, and emotions went through my mind in those few seconds that I needed to sort out before I chose my response.

My default program was to respond in the former. Come up with some lame excuse about how I was in charge or how I changed my mind. Something that would cement my position as mother, authority figure, and the boss. I don't know why that was my default programming; that was the response I wanted to give. I had a fear of losing control, and I wanted to remain in my comfort zone. I'm good at being the boss.

Yet, the look on my daughter's face said that I needed to respond differently. It said that we had been here before; I had disappointed her or promised her something in the past and dismissed it in the wrong way when I broke that promise. It was as if her face was saying, "Mommy, please don't do this to me again." It broke my heart.

I needed **courage** because my programming was telling me to respond one way, yet my instincts were telling me to do the complete opposite. I needed the courage to step outside my comfort zone, which is usually daunting for anyone.

Courage is the quality of mind or spirit that enables a person to face difficulty, danger, pain, or uncertainty without fear. It's about acting bravely in the face of adversity, whether that's standing up for what you believe in, facing your fears, or taking risks for the greater good. Courage is not the absence of fear but rather the ability to confront and persevere despite it. It's often seen as a noble and admirable trait because it requires strength, resilience, and sometimes self-sacrifice.

The interesting thing about courage is that it does not require a grand event to exhibit itself. Sure, one needs courage for those big scary events like going to war, standing up for yourself or someone else, or facing natural disasters. One also needs courage for the previously mentioned Hallmark moments. But what about everyday life?

We need courage to get through the small things in life. Why did I need courage in this situation and carefully choose my response to my daughter?

Simply put, we need courage to be human.

Courage is an essential aspect of being human because it enables us to navigate the complexities of life, confront challenges, and strive for personal growth and connection. It allows us to express the rainbow of our emotions, discover who we are, and inform our actions.

Courage is essential to our humanity.

In that car with Sofia, the best decision, really the only decision I had to make, was admitting I made a mistake.

Admitting a mistake requires a significant amount of courage. It means facing the fear of consequences for your mistake. Often, a fear of negative consequences is associated with admitting to a mistake. You might worry about damaging your reputation, facing disciplinary action at work, or damaging relationships with others.

Courage means taking accountability, acknowledging your role in a positive or negative situation, and being willing to face the outcomes. This includes admitting mistakes, making amends when necessary, and actively working toward solutions or improvement. Essentially, it's about owning up to your actions and their impact on yourself and others rather than deflecting blame or making excuses.

Showing your vulnerability and acknowledging your imperfections requires courage. We humans connect with each other not through our perfections but through our imperfections. Exposing your flaws or weaknesses can be uncomfortable, especially if you fear judgment or criticism from others. It can be uncomfortable to admit you don't know something. We all have egos, we all have pride. Admitting to a mistake means putting your ego and pride aside. It can be challenging to admit when you're wrong, especially if you have a strong attachment to being perceived as competent or infallible, as I used to.

Going against your programming takes courage. First, it takes courage to identify and admit that you have programming that doesn't serve you. Second, it takes courage to take the steps to correct it. One's programming is like habits; it's how our unconscious mind reacts because it's been conditioned to do so. We can have good or bad habits, and we can have good or bad programming. The reason we want to change our programming is because we want a different outcome; we want to be better, behave better, and we want a boost. What is more human than that?

Admitting a mistake, taking accountability, displaying vulnerability, and changing programming are all elements of overcoming. All traits of being human. All requiring courage.

So, sitting in that car with Sofia, what did I decide to do?

I awkwardly turned around in the car's driver's seat so I could look Sofia directly in the eye instead of through the rearview mirror. I used my best, soothing mom-voice and said, "Sofia, I'm sorry. You're right. I know I made a promise to you, and I broke it. Today didn't work out the way I thought. I made a mistake, and I am very sorry."

I had the courage to go against my programming, take responsibility, admit my mistakes, and show my vulnerability. Courage.

I watched Sofia's face for a response. She took a moment, which in reality was probably only one second, but felt longer. Her face began to soften, her eyebrows moving from their upward knit to a normal position. Her face transformed from a look of disappointment to calm. She started to smile.

In that instant, I knew I made the right decision.

"Mommy," Sofia said, "it's okay. I understand."

As the quote from Alexander Pope says, *"To err is human, to forgive is divine."* Thank you for forgiving me, Sofia.

I shared my vulnerability, and we connected on that level. I accepted responsibility, and Sofia knew the situation wasn't her fault. I set an example for my daughter of how to admit to making a mistake. I demonstrated courage.

The interesting thing is the reason I wanted to respond differently was based on my programming and my desire to remain in control. I argue that by exhibiting courage and sharing my vulnerability, I did remain in control. Instead of Sofia overreacting or crying, I provided her with a safe space, and she forgave me. We were able to go about our evening. We strengthened our relationship. We both felt good. Control was maintained, all due to the courage to do something differently.

We quickly exited the car and hugged, then went about the rest of our evening.

This event, which lasted no more than two minutes, has informed my parenting style since. I freely admit that I make mistakes in front of my kids. I approach their mistakes with empathy and as an opportunity to grow and learn. I apologize to them when needed. They know that if I make a promise, I will keep it (especially if we pinky swear). I also tell them when I cannot promise something if I'm unsure I can make it happen. Not only does this event inform my parenting, but it also informs my communication and interaction with everyone.

Finding the courage to be human changed my life. It turns out that being more human made me more human.

About the Author

Carmen Ventrucci is multiple #1 best international book author, real estate investor, and business communication expert. She thrives in conversation and helping business grow by setting the intention behind communication. Her newest passion is coaching girls' youth hockey. Carmen, her husband, five children, and two dogs love to go camping, and have toured the USA in their camper. Carmen can be reached at carmen.ventrucci@gmail.com.

Cesar R. Espino, MBA

CHAPTER SEVENTEEN

DISCOVER THE COURAGE WITHIN

Being courageous is a fundamental and essential aspect of overcoming anything, and I can guarantee you that at one point in your life, you had to show some **courage**. Now, if you are telling yourself, "No, that is not me; I have never been courageous," then you are in the right place. By reading this book and this chapter, you will learn and further understand why courage, regardless of your current age, is a critical factor in moving forward in your personal and professional life. First, let us understand the meaning or definition of courage. Per merriam-webster.com, the definition of courage is: *mental or moral strength to venture, persevere, and withstand danger, fear, or difficulty.*

When you understand the meaning and see that there is a mental or moral element to create imagination (venture), continue to grow as an individual (persevere), have the strength to push forward regardless of the pain and decisions made (withstand danger), and in allowing yourself to be calculated in facing the fear and doing it anyway (fear or difficulty) are things we faced on our daily lives. Think about it: from day one of your existence, you had to go through something, like facing the fear of not doing anything to crawling, to withstanding the danger of crawling to taking your first step. Everything here was an act of courage, and if you never took those steps, never built what was needed inside of you, then you would have never progressed in life and into the next stage in your life, in this case, being a kid of one, two, or three years.

With this simple example, and as I think of my life, I can now see how many moments in life I had to show an act of courage, even if, at that moment, I did not realize it or see it that way. I also can think of those around me, like my mom, who had her own moments of courage and bravery. And before I tell you about some of my own experiences in life, I want to tell you about my mom's act of courage. Part of that is because we also need to understand that those who are so close to you have a direct connection and influence on what goes on in your life. In other words, what other people near you do can and will create a ripple effect in your life trajectory. For some of us, that could be good, and for others, that could be bad.

I was born in Mexico City in 1980, and as a kid, I saw

my mom do many things that I would describe as acts of courage. One of the biggest things that took place was the day that my mom decided to leave Mexico and migrate to the United States for a better life. Now, I am not sure how long she had been planning this or when she decided to take this huge step, and I do not even know if she recognizes this moment as being brave or seeing it as a huge act of courage. Three months after my 4th birthday, my mom decided to leave her family behind to go after that American dream and provide a better life for her family. She left my older brother (two years older) and me behind with my grandmom (her mom). While this was hard on me, and so much was going on through my head, questioning so many things as to why she left me, this chapter is too small for me to talk about it (you can find the full story at *You Can Overcome Anything! Even When the World Says "NO"),* I cannot even imagine the pain, and lonely days and nights she had to go through.

I have a soon-to-be twenty-eight-year-old daughter, and I cannot imagine leaving her behind at just four years old. Yet my mom did, and this was an act of courage that changed the trajectory of our lives. I am sure my mom embarked on an unknown journey, one where she had little to no money, had no legal documentation, and had to migrate and cross the border illegally into Los Angeles, California. She tried to find a job as an illegal immigrant to survive for herself and also to find the means to send money to Mexico for my older brother, grandma, and I. Talk about making that initial choice and decision. I guess I will never understand how that thought process took place in her mind as I have never had that choice. Remember that the choices and decisions we make today will impact the quality of life that we have tomorrow. If we feel it was not the right choice, we can pivot immediately and make a new choice or decision; the key is not to get stuck and keep moving forward.

Now, do not get me wrong, I am an immigrant myself, having to cross the border illegally and also living some horrifying things along my journey (again, more on this in my very first book), except I never had to make a choice to leave my kids and country behind and come to a new country as my mom did. When I migrated to the United States at the age of ten, I was just a kid, and the choice to come here was made for me. All I had to do was say *goodbye* to my elementary friends and tell them *I was going to the other side,* to *America,* and just wait for the time to come and for my entire family to migrate. As I think about it now, this was never my choice, this choice was probably made the minute my mom decided to leave (six years prior), and the minute she figured out that the opportunity for us was in Los Angeles and not in Mexico.

While my mom was away figuring out the life she would give me, my grandmom was taking care of me, and this reminded me of what Abraham Lincoln said: *"All that I am or hope to be, I owe to my angel mother."* While my mom is still alive and my grandmom, who I saw as my *"mom"* as well, has since passed away several years ago, I am blessed to have had two of them on my side. Both showed great courage, and those sacrifices made a huge difference in my life and who I am today.

"All That I am or Hope Ever to be I Get From My Mother."
~ Abrahma Lincon

Now, you might be wondering how those acts from my mom made a difference in my life. Well, to begin, it gave me an opportunity that was so far away from me in Mexico and opened other great opportunities for me while in this great nation. Opportunities that perhaps I did not have the courage to see through and fulfill, and during that ride called life, I've made so many mistakes that I now see and recognize as life lessons. See, you need to understand that our so-called mistakes are only mistakes if you do not learn from them, and if you keep making them repeatedly. When you see something wrong, you rectify it and do something about it; you become more powerful, and that so-called mistake becomes a life lesson. Also, sometimes our human nature is that we are so afraid of the unknown, or we do not want to get uncomfortable, or even worse, we are always looking for opportunities to be dressed as a shiny object, pleasant and bright when in reality it may be disguised as ugly, uncomfortable, hard work, discipline, courage, and therefore we do not act and or take that opportunity. Believe me, I have been there, and my advice to you is to recognize that the opportunity is out there, do not allow fear to take that from you, and go after it.

For instance, I had seen an opportunity for quite some time, and because it was disguised, I was afraid and backed down from it. I was working for a top global logistics company in their corporate office. I had a great salary paying me over six figures, bonuses, and full benefits, and I traveled all over the states, was comfortable, and loved my job. However, something deep down did not feel right, and part of me was telling me that this was not for me. It was like something deep down was telling me to jump. But because I was comfortable and afraid of the unknown, I froze and did not pull the trigger to leave the job and do my own thing. When I had these feelings, I had already done several real estate deals and had been on the investing side for at least 10+ years. I had also done some other business, so I knew what that was and meant. The challenge is that I was never fully committed, and because of that, there was no consistent flow of money coming in through my investing or side jobs. By this time, I also held a master's degree in business administration, so part of my mind was telling me to continue the path of an employee. You know that path that is engraved in our heads since we are in elementary school, especially for someone like me, a poor, immigrant kid whose second language is English, for sure the idea of going to school, getting good grades, graduating, getting a good corporate job, and retiring was screaming out loud in my mind. Heck, I had all of that and more going for me. Do not get me wrong; I had everything that many companies will want: educated with an MBA, experience, determination, and hardworking, except I also had seen one too many times people getting laid off after many years (in some cases 20+ years) in working for the same company. So, the other part of me was saying, "Cesar, you need to take that leap of faith; just jump."

While this looked like it was good, I froze and did not make that move until after seven to eight months, when the idea came into play for me to do so. Remember how I mentioned that our decisions and choices today will determine our quality of life tomorrow? Well, I can honestly say that this is one of those times where if I had taken that decision early on when the idea came to mind, I would certainly be in a different place. Who knows, maybe ahead or behind? In the end, everything we do has consequences, and at the same time, we cannot live in the past. We need to learn from our past and not dwell on it. That said, while I did not build the courage to do it then, and I've certainly lost people, things, opportunities, once I have built the courage and determination to take the leap of faith, things change. Once I decided to make that choice, to pivot and make it, and be aware that I would be out of a job and on my own, it was game on. That has been one of my biggest courageous moments in life, leaving everything behind and venturing into the unknown, yet I did it.

Many probably have been there, and you can relay, or many of you are thinking of doing that, and I can tell you that you must build that courage and determination and take that leap, at least do it once in your life, and if you are afraid, know that is okay and still do it anyways. If you do not take that leap of faith, leave that job, open that business, ask that guy or girl out, or burn the boats, you will live with regret and will always go back and ask yourself, why? Except the minute you do take that leap and build that courage, you will be grateful you did because you will not live with regret, and if it did not work out, now you know what not to do next time. Again, every decision has a consequence, and if it is not the outcome you were looking forward to, remember you can pivot; just don't stay down.

"Life is full of adventures and secrets... things you do not expect, yet at the end of the day, it is how you react to those cases and what you do about it... it may not be clear or shiny, but don't let the circumstances take the best of you." ~ Cesar R. Espino

Let's talk about life adventures and how they can be scary and rewarding at the same time. Of course, once you face that fear, you will have the courage to take the next step. Now, you might be asking yourself what adventure can be frightful and what determination you need to move forward. This can be different from person to person, yet I want to speak to you about my scary adventure a few years ago. Picture this: something you really want to do, a place you've wanted to go, except before you embark on that adventure, you are uncertain, afraid, do not know what to expect, or even how to go about it, all you have is the hunch of wanting to do it.

This happened to me several years back when I had planned for the first time in my life to go on a trip to Europe all by myself, specifically Paris, France. I went to Paris in 2016; however, I went with my girlfriend then. This occasion was different, as I was going by myself with no real agenda, and I did not even know anyone; I just wanted to experience something new and have an adventure. This may not seem scary, yet I can guarantee you that if you have never traveled by yourself to a country across the world from your home city or a place where you do not even speak the language or know anyone, it can be intimidating and scary at the same time.

As soon as I got to Paris, I was excited, yet at the same time, I did not know what to do or to expect. The nights got lonely, tourist places were sad, and taking selfie pictures or asking others to take a picture of me was embarrassing. There were so many emotions; some days, I literally had emotional meltdowns, where melancholy kicked in, and tears dropped down my eyes.

I tell you this story so you can understand that as soon as I purchased that ticket, boarded that plane, and arrived in Paris, I showed courage and committed myself. Regardless of the emotional rollercoaster, I built enough courage to embark on this journey. I also learned many things about myself and experienced new things that I would have never seen without this trip.

Well, guess what? After doing that, I tried it again, and this time, I went to Puerto Rico and then forced myself to go on a seven-day cruise, embarked on the cruise ship without knowing anyone, and went all in. Now, this time around, on my first night on the cruise, with over 3000 strangers, I broke into tears, and I questioned myself, "What am I doing? Why am I here all by myself?" This was probably scarier than being alone on land, yet I was courageous enough to take this trip. I've learned more about myself and learned that while it is nice, I do not need anyone on my side to enjoy life and see new things or need anyone to travel. I've learned how to meet new people, make connections, talk about my business, who I am, and what's best. I appreciated life from an entirely new different perspective. So, guess what? Because of that courageous move several years back, I have since gone on two cruises all by myself, not knowing anyone. I have traveled to many places by myself, like Japan, France, Italy, Puerto Rico, Alaska, Colombia, etc., and life has been great and a blessing. I have learned to treat myself to fancy dinners and sit at a table all by myself while others are with their significant other, family, or friends, and still enjoy it to the fullest. I have learned to love myself more than anything, something we all need to do. I have learned how not to be afraid and go on that trip or adventure because, quite honestly, we are here today, and we are gone tomorrow. We do not know when we will have our last moment of breath, so why not have the courage to do anything we want in our lives? Because of this, I am no longer afraid and get excited when booking a solo trip anywhere in the world. I am ready, and I've built that courage to be okay by myself and see what life has to offer.

What I would like you to take away from my stories and the other authors' stories is to create courageous moments in your life and create them to be unique to you as we are all different, and what might seem small to someone else is huge for you. Go after it and get it.

- Have the courage to make a positive change in your life by changing your habits or daily routines.
- Have the courage to ask that other person out.
- Have the courage to leave your job to pursue something bigger and greater.
- Have the courage to take the leap of faith and start that business you always wanted.
- Have the courage to travel the world all by yourself.
- Have the courage to go to a fancy dinner all by yourself.
- Have the courage to go to the movies by yourself.
- Have the courage to start loving you, even if no one gives you any external validation.
- Have the courage to create the person you want to be because if you are not growing, you are slowly dying deep down.

- Have the courage to go after all that you want to go after, and remember that with courage, *You Can Overcome Anything!*

About the Author

Cesar R. Espino is the creator of You Can Overcome Anything! Podcast Show, You Can Overcome Anything Book Series, a real estate investor, mind coach, business consultant, and multiple #1 best international book author. His passion and highest intention are to empower, inspire, and motivate others to reach their full potential. Cesar offers a variety of tools and services to help people improve their current situation. He is creating opportunities for people to have a chance at life regardless of people's background and current situation.

Website: www.CesarRespino.com
www.linktree.com/espinoc
Podcast:
https://podcasts.apple.com/us/podcast/you-can-overcome-anything-podcast-show/id1497917624?uo=4

ABOUT THE AUTHOR

Cesar R. Espino was born in Mexico City when the country had one of the largest foreign debts and was going through a financial crisis. Not only was he born into a poor family, but he was also born to just one parent (his mom) and never met his biological father. As a kid, Cesar lived with his grandmother, mom, and older brother, living in a room or what he called his house that was just about 200 square feet. This place had no running water, no floor. He lived and slept directly on top of dirt, with no insulation, and was made of sheet metal and plywood. He lived in this house holding four of them until he was just a few months to four years old. Around the time his mom took the leap of faith, she left her family behind and migrated to the United States to chase the American Dream and support her family across boundaries. This became a pivotal moment in Cesar's life as this forced him to start working at an early age (at four) just to survive and put some food on the table. Throughout his life journey, he has overcome many different obstacles. Today Cesar R. Espino's passion is to empower, educate, and inspire many through his experiences and life lessons. Cesar has a Master's Degree in Business Administration, has worked for several worldwide companies, held positions in corporate America, and is an Author of the Book *You Can Overcome Anything! Even When the World Says" NO"* is a Co-Author of the Book *Dare to be Authentic Vol.5 Let Yourself Prosper*, International Author of the Book *Puedes Superar Cualquier Cosa! Incluso Cuando El Mundo Dice "NO,"* Co-Author of the Book *How We Became Entrepreneurs,*

Follow Our Leads: Book 1, and many other books, Real Estate Investor, Real Estate Mentor, Podcast Host of the Show **You Can Overcome Anything! Podcast Show** and, most importantly, a son, father, and grandfather.

Cesar offers a variety of programs to help people improve their current situation, educate them, and provide a way to have their own business. Cesar's is creating opportunities for people to have a chance at life regardless of people's background and current situation. He is able to do this through his many different programs and experiences in multiple areas.

Such areas of:

- Real Estate Investing
- Best Selling Books
- NLP (Mind and Life Coach)
- Mentoring
- Business Consulting
- Self-Development Events
- Live Public Speaking, Podcast, and News
- Life Insurance and Infinite Banking

        www.facebook.com/cesar.espino.1297
        www.instagram.com/cesarrespino
        www.CesarRespino.com
        www.linkedin.com/in/cesar-espino
        @cesarrespino

READ THE BOOK THAT STARTED IT ALL

You Can Overcome Anything! Even When The World Says "NO" - Cesar Espino's passion for motivation and his drive to succeed go back to his roots. Born in Mexico City into a society of poverty and very little hope, it took years for him to recognize that a larger purpose had been set in front of him, one that he would chase for the rest of his life.

You Can Overcome Anything is as much a recounting of Cesar's determined journey as it is a reminder that when you have a dream and refuse to give up, anything is possible.

OTHERS GREAT BOOKS TO READ

- You Can Overcome Anything! Vol. 1 Despite The Barriers In Life
- You Can Overcome Anything! Vol. 2 When You Exercise The Mind
- You Can Overcome Anything! Vol. 3 With A Definite Purpose
- You Can Overcome Anything! Vol. 4 When You Walk With Certainty
- You Can Overcome Anything! Vol. 5 When You Have Irresistible Influence
- You Can Overcome Anything! Vol. 6 When You Believe
- You Can Overcome Anything! Vol. 7 With Love
- You Can Overcome Anything! Vol. 8 With Integrity
- You Can Overcome Anything! Vol. 9 With Clarity
- You Can Overcome Anything! Vol. 10 With Awareness
- You Can Overcome Anything! Vol. 11 With Forgiveness
- You Can Overcome Anything! Vol. 12 With Faith
- Keys to Wholesaling
- Follow Our Leads: How We Became Entrepreneurs
- Follow Our Leads: What It's Like Being Entrepreneurs
- Follow Our Leads: How We Stay Entrepreneurs
- Todo Chido Un Nuevo Comienzo
- Puedes Superar Cualquier Cosa! Incluso Cuando El Mundo Dice Que "NO"

Manufactured by Amazon.ca
Bolton, ON